# TRAUMA
# AND
# ECSTASY

ALEX ABRAHAM

# TRAUMA AND ECSTASY

## HOW PSYCHEDELICS MADE MY LIFE WORTH LIVING

**TRAUMA AND ECSTASY**
How Psychedelics Made My Life Worth Living

FIRST EDITION

ISBN  978-1-5445-4158-7  Hardcover
       978-1-5445-4156-3  Paperback
       978-1-5445-4157-0  Ebook
       978-1-5445-4159-4  Audiobook

*For CA, even when we fight*

*MN, for being there*

*My family*

*And for all the survivors of childhood sexual abuse*

# Contents

# Prologue

I've never liked bikes. Something about not being on my own two feet has always made me nervous. And even in the best-case scenario, the bike seat always seems to ride up in that weird area right behind my balls.

But I was riding a bike in the Netherlands when my life changed.

It was a perfect summer day—cool with a clear sky, a nice breeze, as sunny as it was ever going to get up there. It was 2017, and I was twenty-three years old, had just graduated college, and was ending a multi-continent study abroad turned backpacking trip that I knew was the end of the road before full-time employment.

While I would have told everyone I was still having a great time, as the trip wore on, I was struggling with anxiety more than usual.

I was determined to make the trip a success. And to me success meant doing as much as I could as quickly as I could. So it only took me a day and a half to do what the tourist websites recommended doing over four days. After I saw or did something cool, I would spend about five minutes appreciating whatever it was...and then it was right back to the next item on the agenda.

Moving so fast made it impossible to stay in a routine. Never a good sleeper, I insisted on staying in the grungiest and most crowded hostels to try to save money. I'd also lost enough weight from my already thin frame that I had to buy new clothes.

By the time I got to the Netherlands, I was so exhausted that I thought about leaving early. But I only had four days left before I had to be in London to then fly to California for a friend's wedding. I knew that if I left Europe now, I'd be mad at myself for quitting. That was the lens through which I saw everything: not so much about leaning into what felt good but instead doing everything I could to avoid feeling bad, whether in the present moment or in an imagined future.

I had planned to stay in Amsterdam, but it was packed. Everyone in the hostel seemed to be there to do drugs. So after a last-minute recommendation by a fellow backpacker, I decided on Texel, an island in the north that had some cool-looking sand dunes and seemed like it could help me relax and that I'd heard was best explored by bike.

I hustled to catch the ferry and got to Texel late in the evening. The next morning, there were almost no bikes available to rent. When I was finally able to find one, the seat was too far back for me to ride comfortably. I'd always felt more at peace in motion and was in a hurry to get going. I tried to fix the seat, but I couldn't figure it out and was too stubborn to ask someone for help. So after a couple minutes of cussing under my breath, I gave up and just started riding, stretching myself out and arching my back forward as far as I could.

Despite being uncomfortable, I rode that bike around the whole island.

There wasn't one moment when I knew something was wrong, but when I hopped off the bike seat late that afternoon, something felt different—like I had clipped somewhere in my pelvic region, between my scrotum and my butt, the very danger zone I'd always worried about. It felt the same as when I hit my funny bone, an odd feeling, but it didn't really hurt, so I wasn't concerned. I went to bed assuming it would be gone by the morning.

It wasn't. I still felt sort of a tingling sensation, and I decided I wasn't going to get on a bike again. Not really feeling the Netherlands anymore, I headed to England early.

After a couple days of walking around, the tingling had not disappeared at all—if anything, it seemed to have gotten worse. I also noticed I started having to take a piss more than usual. I had no idea what the problem was, but I decided I should try to find a doctor before my flight.

I had never seen a doctor in a foreign country before. I ended up in a sketchy, cash-only walk-in clinic on the fringe of the city. The doctor, with his thick English accent, was cool but seemed to think I was crazy.

"You'll be fine," he said with a smile, putting his right hand under his pants inseam for effect. "Those seats can really ride up on ya." He gave me some muscle relaxants, patted me on the shoulder, and sent me on my way.

I flew to San Francisco the next day before heading to wine country, where I got to hang out with a bunch of people I had not seen in ages. I stopped worrying about whatever was going on "down there" for a couple of days. But I couldn't help but notice as the reception got underway that I was still a little uncomfortable. I kinda felt like I had to take a piss, almost like my bladder couldn't quite decide. And I didn't have all the usual feeling of sensations when I did urinate, like I couldn't quite tell if I had finished.

Luckily, most people there—including me—were pretty buzzed. Between the singing and the back slapping, no one noticed I was spending a little extra time in the bathroom.

That wedding was the last event where I felt quasi-normal.

I had no idea it was the canary in the coal mine for what was to come.

# The Day My Dick Stopped Working

S hortly after I get back from the wedding, I move to Salt Lake City, Utah, from northern Virginia, where I grew up, to start my new job.

It now feels like I'm sitting on a golf ball that has somehow been lobbed into my rectum. I think it could be bacteria or some other kind of infection. On the drive across the country, I start feeling a tightness in my lower abdomen and a now urgent feeling like I need to piss. I am also at times experiencing what seems to be a spasmic burning somewhere inside my asshole that takes all my willpower not to try to scratch away.

Driving across the country is also the first time I wake up in the middle of the night desperately needing to urinate. Even after I go it feels incomplete, that I somehow still have to go again, when only the smallest of trickles is leaking out.

I find another doctor as soon as I get to Utah. He agrees I probably picked up some sort of infection on my travels and writes me a prescription for antibiotics. "God knows what goes on in some of these places," he says.

Work starts. In addition to having to piss all the time, I am now having trouble shitting. Everything is backed up like a traffic jam.

I have to arch my back forward and strain my muscles to try to push it all out, which only seems to make things worse. I have to look down to get any sense of what is coming out of me—tiny lumpy pellets that look more like pebbles in an ocean painting than something that belongs in a toilet

At the same time, masturbating has started not to feel great. I can still get an erection, but actually jacking off is tighter and less enjoyable, like I am forcing something, in much the same way as shitting. And afterward, there is sometimes a burning sensation in my shaft that makes me put my hands up and want to back away.

I come up with all sorts of shame-related reasons why this could be happening. Maybe I've been jacking off too hard or too much? Whatever it is, I am freaked the fuck out. I spend hours surfing the web, self-diagnosing myself with everything under the sun: a hernia, a pinched nerve, an infected bicycle.

I start bringing an empty water bottle to bed with me so I don't wake my roommates on my many trips back and forth to the bathroom. I decide I can't live with people right now and get my own place.

I also find a new doctor. We take turns using a stool to simulate my position on the bike. He says in order to assess the situation, he needs to inspect "down there." I put my hands on the exam table, pull my pants down, and face away from him, already grossed out as I hear him snap on the latex glove.

When he goes in, I can feel my muscles clench up in a way that he agrees seems strong. He's not sure what is wrong but recommends staying on antibiotics and sends me to pelvic floor physical therapy.

The physical therapist goes in with the idea that using her hand to massage different "trigger points" will help them relax. As she is massaging, she says, "Wow."

It is not the good "Wow."

At certain spots, I yell loud enough that she has to reassure her suite neighbors that everything is okay. The closer she gets to my asshole, the worse things seem to be.

I decide to keep seeing her every week because I don't know what else to do.

Amid all this, I am lonely. I have a work connection in Utah but don't know anyone there my age. I have never been on a formal date in my life, but I start downloading dating apps and compulsively swiping, even on girls I know are not a good fit for me—like some part of me knows this could be it for my dick.

One Friday, bored after work, I match with a girl who suggests drinks that night. She invites me to her place. Right as we are taking things to the next level, I look down and realize my dick isn't moving. I've never had a problem getting it up before, but now it's lights out. My dick has died! Panicked, I start performing oral sex on her to try to stall. After a while, there's still no sign of movement.

"What's wrong?" she asks, lying on her bed, naked, in the dark.

"Uh, I've been taking some antibiotics, and, uh, I think I took too many and, uh, with the drink we had, I'm just not...I think I've gotta go," I say, fumbling with my keys on the way out.

I go to bed in shock, hoping that when I wake up tomorrow things will be different.

They aren't.

I have to stroke for several minutes to get something that is still so flaccid it cannot really be called an erection. I mostly stop waking up with morning wood, but on the rare days I do, it is shriveled and shrunken looking. At times I feel plenty of libido, but my dick won't move, like wires are getting crossed. Other times, I feel no sex drive at all.

The spasmic pain every time I do try to jack off and afterward doesn't help. Nor does the extra urine that has started trickling out every time I piss, sometimes as late as when I am washing my hands getting ready to go back to work.

I decide I have a deep infection similar to Lyme disease. I take months of the strongest antibiotics possible until I start getting skin rashes from a fungal infection and my mom has to almost force me to stop.

Day to day, I'm not in agony, but I feel nonstop discomfort. Some days are worse than others, but the tightness never ever goes away, like a clenched fist in my pelvic region, with excruciating pain after shitting, jacking off, and sometimes even urinating.

It becomes clear that everything is related. The weaker the erection, the more extra piss comes out, the worse it hurts to shit. And occasionally comes the burning, the throbbing, the stabbing radiating from somewhere deep inside my asshole. I have no control.

I start taking Advil every day because it makes me feel slightly better. Hot baths help a little, but the second I get out the relaxation disappears like I never even took one. I need a prescription-grade muscle relaxant to fall asleep at night.

Even with drugs, I always seem to wake up with an urgency to piss at about the four-hour mark. I am anxious, alert, and my pelvis tight enough that when I do wake up it is hard to calm down enough to go back to sleep. I don't sleep more than five or so hours at a time over the next several years.

One night, I wake up suddenly because it feels like fire is radiating from my pelvis. I can barely breathe, sit still, or formulate a thought it hurts so much. I am still half asleep and in shock, so I immediately take my muscle relaxant and Advil and start a bath. By the time I'm in the bath and have woken up a bit, the pain is completely gone.

This happens several times over the next couple of years. Each time it goes away almost immediately after I wake up, and each time seems just as strange as the last.

Over time, the rest of my body starts to feel off kilter. Everything from my glutes to my back to my shoulders to my neck to my jaw starts to feel tight. I can tell my posture is off. I find myself feeling like I'm going to fall over every time I run. I am being held together by string, having turned into an old man overnight.

I'm also living like an old man. I am in bed before nine o'clock, both because I'm exhausted and because I know I'll wake up in the middle of the night. I have almost entirely cut out alcohol because it makes me feel like I have to piss even more than I already do. In some ways I'm grateful to be away from all my friends because I don't have to justify why I've turned into a recluse.

I try pot a couple of times, but if anything it makes my anxiety about my symptoms worse.

I wonder if it could be a diet issue, but after a month of eating the blandest food possible, there is no change.

Life is much less exciting being impotent. *Why am I wearing nice clothes to work?* I wonder one morning. *Why bother staying in shape? What's the point of even going to a bar or on a date right now—what's the best that can happen?*

I continue seeing doctor after doctor and one physical therapist after another.

They all ask me about stress, so I try mediating, vacationing, swimming, journaling, yoga, saunas, weight lifting (I fall over trying to deadlift), and reading deep philosophical shit. There is no improvement.

I struggle to pass the time, especially on weekends. I start making lists of things I need to be doing—even things as simple as reminding myself to read a book—because if I sit still for too long, I have to ponder my situation.

Because my erectile dysfunction is what I'm most worried about, my mom suggests an ED specialist.

Within the initial ninety seconds, the first guy announces that it's a confidence issue and he can get anyone an erection. He gestures toward my junk and adds, "He just needs to remember what he's supposed to be doing."

He prescribes a large dose of daily Viagra. I am now a walking erection—except I have to look down to be able to tell I have one. There is no connection between me and my dick. The "erection," if you can call it that, is still kind of flaccid and unnatural looking. And even on Viagra, jacking off is the same level of unpleasant.

I switch doctors. We start with a penile injection to see "what's going on," despite me telling him I have already tried Viagra. My dick gets much larger but is still clearly flaccid. He inspects it from every angle and announces, "Something is wrong here."

"I know," I tell him with frustration in my voice. "What do you think the problem is?"

"I'm not sure," he says. "But I mostly do implants."

"You mean like on my dick?"

"Well," he says, "I've never put one on someone so young before." He's almost leering at me when he says this. I'm standing in front of him, naked from the waist down, with half a hard-on. My eyebrows raise, and he mumbles something about being concerned about the liability.

We do not schedule a follow-up appointment. The right side of my dick remains blue at the injection site for weeks. I stop seeing ED guys.

I find an infectious disease specialist and do extensive blood-work. I am ruled out for rheumatoid arthritis, viruses, parasites, and many other diseases. The MRI shows some inflammation but no structural damage of any kind.

Another doctor is convinced I have an STD. He seems to almost not hear me when I tell him I've already been tested.

"There's no shame in it," he says. "I did some pretty wild stuff when I was young too." He then goes into graphic detail about a youthful sexual encounter he had, seeming to think that if he confides in me, I will confide in him. I again test negative for all STDs.

He prescribes valium suppositories, tiny packets that I insert rectally. They are the first thing I try that I see any sort of improvement. I have slightly less urgency and slightly better bowel movements, libido, and sleep. I still do not feel anywhere even resembling normal, but the suppositories make it so I can at least occasionally think about other things.

I start taking valium like they are candy and carry them with me everywhere. It takes all my willpower to not take one all the time, every day.

I don't talk to anyone about this, other than my mom, somewhat out of embarrassment but mostly out of alarm. When I go back home to Virginia to visit friends, I drink a little bit to keep up appearances and then get uncomfortable enough that I have to go to the bar bathroom to shove valium up my ass.

Amid all this, I endlessly swipe through dating apps, trying to find validation for my shrinking self-esteem. Occasionally, I go on dates because I don't have anything else to do and I want to feel normal.

One night, I match with a girl and meet her at a dive bar. She is very forward in what she wants us to do later. I know that won't go well, so I pretend not to understand and make up an excuse about why I am busy in a way that visibly perplexes and later offends her.

Another time, I match with Ashley. She invites me on a date, and for some reason I decide to go. I take valium right before and try to forget how uncomfortable I am. Ashley has a cute smile, and the date is, oddly enough, a great distraction. We discover we are both Utah transplants who like hiking, documentaries, and Indian food.

Intimacy is an issue from the beginning. She is touchy-feely, and even before my pelvic problems, I was very much not. She often wants to kiss or hang out more, and I push back. Sex is obviously a problem—mainly that we never have it. I have to take multiple valiums to get hard enough just to get a painful blowjob. Often my dick doesn't work well enough to even do that. I tell her I'm having back issues and while she doesn't seem super concerned, I am frustrated.

In the beginning, she seems to really like me. I start getting suspicious of why that is and accuse her of only wanting to hang out because I pay for everything.

As time goes on and as my dick continues not to work, I tell her that the only reason we're together is because we live in Utah and not a bigger, more fun state. I am so mired in myself that I genuinely don't see how this is mean.

One day she has had enough and says we are done, telling me, "You make me feel so bad about myself."

After that, I mostly stop going on dates.

The longer this goes on, the harder time I have imagining a scenario where it will ever go away. The tension feels like a part of me now. The first thing I do when I go anywhere is scan where the bathrooms are, often without even realizing it. And even when I have just gone to the bathroom, I always feel like I need to go.

I still believe doctors can heal me from this chronic, long-term health issue. When I don't go see doctors, I think that I am not doing anything to help myself fix this.

After a couple of failed visits, my whole body starts tensing up every time I sit on the antiseptic examination table in a gown, explaining my situation to a new urologist.

They all seem to congregate around two extremes: "This will go away soon," or "This may be a chronic condition that you will have to live with forever."

I am twenty-four years old when, five minutes into meeting me, an overweight MD with bad skin declares me permanently erectile deficient. My fists clench as soon as I can tell they have no idea and are just making shit up.

"How could I possibly have permanent erectile dysfunction?" I yell.

"It's been over a year. Why would my dick just start working again?" I snap to others.

Most of them quickly revert to "I am a doctor and you are not" logic.

Several of them ask a version of "What do *you* think is wrong with you?"

Another asks, "Have you tried relaxing?"

There are almost never any follow-up appointments. I end several of them by informing the doctor in question that he (they are almost all men) is "a fucking idiot" and slamming the door behind me.

I go under and get a Botox injection in my ass. It does not help.

One guy claims to do pelvic floor surgery. The reviews are so traumatizing I have to go outside and get some air after reading them.

My physical therapist suggests talk therapy. The idea that this burning physical health issue could have an emotional component, or that it could be solved by talking about it for sixty minutes a week on a couch, is crazy to me.

I go to therapy sporadically anyway. I do not look hard for a good therapist. I downplay the problem the second I get in there. My tone of voice stays flat the entire time. I never cry.

I seem to know exactly what to say for them to tell me I am going to be fine. I try to convince myself of this too. We sit on couches with our eyes closed and practice mindfulness exercises together. After a couple of sessions with each of several different therapists, I stop going.

My physical therapist also recommends acupuncture. The acupuncturist is sure she can help me. She sticks needles right in my asshole, starts cupping different parts of my body, and prescribes a detailed herb regimen. Acupuncture does relax me, and occasionally I fall asleep in there. It doesn't do anything for my symptoms, though.

After a couple of sessions, the acupuncturist notes that my pelvis seems just as tight as when we started. This happens a lot. The practitioners are all confident they can help me at the beginning, but not so much later. Just like the doctors, they ask me, "Why do you think you are still here or have not gotten better?" Their tone always makes me feel like I am failing them and myself.

And then, one day while I'm trying to forget how much I have to go to the bathroom, I stumble on a post by the writer Tucker Max talking about his experience with MDMA-assisted psychotherapy. While I have never communicated with Tucker, I've followed his therapeutic journey on social media for years.

Before his piece, I associated psychedelics like mushrooms or LSD with strange hippies in the woods who weren't doing anything with their lives. But that impression came from others. I hadn't actually given the psychedelics themselves much thought at all. I'd never taken or even been offered them. I didn't know many people who had taken them and never in any kind of therapeutic setting.

MDMA, or ecstasy (which is not technically a hallucinogenic/psychedelic), didn't weird me out as much. I had actually done it a couple of times at parties in college, but this seemed different.

Tucker wrote about wearing an eyeshade, with a guide and zen music, in a way that at first almost seemed like satire.

Except he was 100 percent serious talking about how impactful even two MDMA sessions had been for him in working through childhood trauma—and that he would be taking more psychedelics soon. Tucker's piece is so in your face that psychedelics can help heal trauma that I never forget the association.

I read it several times in the following days because it seems interesting. After that, I'm not dismissive of MDMA therapy and decide it could be a real game changer for veterans, rape survivors, and other people with trauma.

But I don't have any of those issues; I just have a strange physical health problem.

I don't discuss Tucker's piece or MDMA therapy with anyone and, after a couple of days, stop consciously thinking about it.

"It's more an art than a science," the physical therapist says as he hands me lubricant and latex to make entry smoother.

At a five-day clinic in California, marketed for those who have failed all other pelvic floor treatments, I am given a curved wooden cargo hook known as "the wand." It is not so different from a backscratcher—except I insert the wand rectally. The idea is that, after the clinic is over, patients can use the wand to massage their own trigger points without help from a physical therapist.

Lying down in the hotel bedroom with a sheet over me, I am steering the wand from side to side like a joystick, letting it linger on different points. It is horrifically painful, even worse than physical therapy. I feel like I am going to die rubbing this wooden object all around my inner anus.

And then physical therapy is over for the day and it's time to go to "Relaxation." About twenty-five men and women of all ages sit in a circle in a converted yoga studio, and I try to avoid eye contact with all of them. The founder tells us that he started this clinic to solve his own pelvic floor issues and that pelvic floor problems have both a physical and emotional component.

After a quick patient Q&A in which butt plugs are mentioned, he clasps his hands and says it is time to get started.

"We are going to use these five days to learn how to relax ourselves," he says. Everyone is handed a yoga mat. His assistant comes around with eye masks. The founder sits in a chair in the middle of our circle. The lights dim.

"It's all going to be okay. It is all going to be fine." He repeats variations of these phrases over and over in a soft, melodic voice. It dawns on me that we are going to do this strange exercise the entire time I am not in physical therapy. *This can't be real*, I think. *How has my life come to this?*

Five days later, the wand is tagged in the airport security line, and I have to explain that it is not a weapon.

I try using it for months. Not only is it painful enough that I have to get in the bath after, but it is also clearly not working, so I give up.

I start having noticeable hip pain, and an MRI shows that I have several labral tears, and both my hips are impinged. The doctor recommends surgery on both hips. My pelvic floor therapist at the time is sure it is related to all my pelvic issues. I am hopeful maybe having the surgeries will somehow change something. It does not.

As my body continues to decline, I become more and more consumed by my career. I decide I want a new job and join a startup in a hot industry that makes me feel important. But from the second I get there, I realize I have made a big mistake. They are dysfunctional enough and it is stressful enough amid all my other problems that I decide to just quit.

When I am unemployed and can't find a new job, I feel adrift with a limp dick. When I stop achieving externally—when that source of self-esteem, of validation, of identity isn't there anymore —I really start to sink. I move back in with my parents.

As the months, even years, go on, it feels as though life is passing me by. I notice people I grew up with and follow on social media have met someone, gotten married, and started families all in the time my dick has not worked.

It is now July 2020, three years after the bike accident. I have found a remote job that I am embarrassed by, but it's better than being unemployed. I have also started seeing a new doctor for pelvic injections that help a little, at least temporarily. He is surprisingly empathetic and genuine. He seems to listen when I speak. He both gets how much of a problem this is and says he is willing to do whatever it takes to help me get better.

I have been meeting with him periodically at his office in New York City, but now he says that I do not seem to be improving and that the best treatment options are here in the city. He doesn't say he won't treat me if I don't move here, but he makes it clear that is what he thinks I should be doing. New York City is the last place I want to be amid COVID-19, but I am desperate and trust him, so I decide to make the move.

At this point I have seen more than twenty doctors, twelve pelvic floor physical therapists, and six acupuncturists around the country. This has proven to be both expensive and useless so far.

Other than my twice-weekly pelvic floor therapy and acupuncture appointments, I have no idea what to do every day or how long

I am going to be in New York. But I have put my foot down—I won't be leaving until I get this fixed.

It is a rough time to be in the city. Everyone I know has left, and everyone still there looks miserable. I try to avoid explaining to anyone why I am up there.

Most indoor activities are closed, and in the winter it starts getting dark at 4:45 p.m. I never totally melt down, but over the years it is a slow decline.

My mom comes to visit me one weekend and observes that I "don't seem to have a great setup here."

"Do you have a better idea?" I snap back.

One day, working in my cramped studio sublet, I come across a podcast from the entrepreneur Tim Ferriss, talking about how MDMA and psilocybin helped him after being serially sexually abused as a young child.

A fan of Tim's, I feel the saddest I have felt in a long time while listening to him talk about his abuse. I attribute it to his story being so horrible. I listen to the podcast and read the transcript several times but don't talk about it with anyone.

In February of 2021, at one of my regularly scheduled doctor's appointments, I tell him that I still have not seen much improvement and want to do more injections.

"The first rule of medicine is to do no harm," he says. "I am 99 percent sure that you are eventually going to be fine. I am going to discharge you as a patient, but I think it would be a good idea to find a talk therapist moving forward."

"What?" I scream at him in shock. "You're quitting? You can't do that!"

He walks out of the exam room, and I find myself almost chasing him down the hallway. He never looks back, and I leave in a huff.

After that, I am stuck. I'm twenty-seven years old. I have been in New York for eight months, and I want to leave and maybe move to Austin, Texas. But I don't think I can go without some sort of plan.

My physical symptoms haven't gotten worse in a long time, but they also have not gotten much better. I know I'm not going to die from this, but I have no idea how it is ever going to get resolved.

And then, walking around Manhattan with my headphones in, I hear him.

# The First Session

After Tucker's piece on MDMA, I start paying close attention to what he has to say about psychedelics. I read his later posts on the topic, begin listening to him on podcasts, and even go as far as searching his name on YouTube to find new interviews.

On one of these interviews, I hear Tucker say, "This experience has been so transformational for me that if someone comes to me looking for a guide, I connect them."

I'm not sure if this is the first time I have heard him say this, but this time it hits different. A light bulb has gone off. I suddenly feel compelled to do MDMA-assisted psychotherapy as soon as I can.

I write to Tucker that I have unresolved trauma and live in New York City and ask him to refer me to a guide. He responds that same day with a proton mail address and a templated email with some code words. Sixty seconds later, I send an email to the address he has given me for my new guide. She responds quickly, and we agree to a phone call on Signal.

I am nervous on the call. I can hear myself speaking in short, clipped sentences, trying to say as little as possible. She introduces herself as Rachel and asks what brought me to this work. I am vague because I'm truly not sure what is bringing me to the work, other than I feel almost called to do it. I don't really have any doubts at this point. I mumble something about my parents not being that great and having some anxiety. That seems to satisfy her. She asks if I have ever done psychedelics before, and I tell her I did molly a couple of times in college at parties. She laughs and says she thinks it will be different this time. She says she would be honored to work with me and that she will be ready to hold space for whatever comes up in my session.

That call is the first time I ever remember saying the word "psychedelics" out loud. I do not mention my pelvis because I don't think I am doing MDMA to heal my pelvis at all but for my day-to-day anxiety. The only thing she seems genuinely concerned about is whether I am on SSRIs or any other medications because SSRIs and MDMA do not mix well. Rachel recommends a couple of supplements to take beforehand, suggests not eating much (if at all) the morning of the session, and tells me to arrive at her apartment on a Saturday at 11:30 a.m. in a month's time. The call lasts maybe fifteen minutes.

I don't tell anyone about this. I go home to Virginia the weekend before to see friends and family, and somehow the fact that I am going to a stranger's house to do drugs the following weekend doesn't come up.

I don't say anything partly because I'm embarrassed. I feel like there is a stigma about psychedelics. I also feel like I don't have any reason to feel this anxious and be doing a trauma-related drug, like there's something wrong with me for having to resort to this measure, particularly at twenty-seven years old. I don't see any of my peers having these sorts of issues, and a part of me judges myself, feeling like I'm unable to pull myself together, that it is my own weakness bringing me to do this.

A couple of days before my session, my internet in my dingy NYC apartment goes out in the middle of the day during a work call I need to be on. I get so mad, screaming at the owner of the apartment when it turns out he has forgotten to pay the bill. The anger goes straight to my back and my neck, and everything tightens up to the point that I have to lie down to calm down. *I can't live like this anymore,* I think. *Something has got to change here.*

On the subway ride to Rachel's apartment, I don't feel nervous. My expectations for what today can accomplish are not high. Several times I wonder why I am going at all. I don't think I have much trauma to work through anyway. I am way more concerned about how my pelvis will ever heal than anything about today.

Rachel buzzes me up, and oddly enough, her space is just how I envisioned it in my head. It looks like a psychiatrist's office, with books on the shelf, cozy furniture, a bed where I will be lying down, and a chair a couple of feet away where she is now sitting with her small dog by her leg.

I know almost nothing about her. She has a couple of decades on me, and outside of today, I am not sure how much we would have in common. It feels like an odd time to be making small talk.

But I trust her almost immediately. She has a casualness about her, not in the sense that she is not taking this seriously but in the "I have done this many times before and seen some shit" kind of way. Everything about her, the setting, the experience feels right.

Rachel tells me that the medicine is designed for people to work through things on their own and she does not usually talk or do much during the session. But she will be there for me if I want to chat, get scared, or need help in any way. She encourages me to say the word "allow" out loud if I ever feel like I am getting stuck or things start getting difficult. She confirms one more time that I am not on any SSRIs or other major medications.

As we are talking, me sitting upright on the bed, her a couple feet away in the chair, she hands me the first 125 mg dose of MDMA. I wash it down with orange juice without hesitation.

She says that in an hour, she will offer me a 75 mg booster that I can take if I want but don't have to. In fact, I don't have to do anything today—there is no pressure at all. "Although," she says with a smile, "I *would* prefer that you don't run off into New York City in the middle of your session."

I mention for the first time that something is off with my pelvis. She says she can't know the specifics, but she thinks it will go away with time and that she has seen all sorts of chronic pain and tension heal from these medicines. Half an hour later, I am still sitting up on the bed talking about how I might move to Austin when I start feeling lightheaded and stop speaking midsentence.

Rachel smiles and asks if I would like to lie down now. I definitely need to lie down now. She hands me a mask. Soft music starts playing in the background. The first things I notice are my jaw and my legs. I am chomping down so hard I am worried my teeth are going to fall out. I remember I have brought a mouthguard and ask her to hand it to me. The second I lie down, my legs start shaking. It is not a violent shaking; it feels like they are moving in slow motion. I can stop them if I want, but it feels good, almost soothing, to have them shake right now.

I ask her why my legs are shaking, and she says that is old, stored trauma coming out of my body and that leg shaking usually indicates a fear response. She says I don't have to shake, but it is good to get it out of my system if I can. She adds that the shaking is a good sign that I am starting to get comfortable with the medicine, that my body is feeling safe enough to start letting go of this somatic trauma.

As the medicine comes on stronger, I start saying all sorts of things.

"I don't think the MDMA is working," I tell her.

She just laughs. "It looks like it's working just fine to me."

"I'm ready for the booster dose," I loudly announce. Then, seconds later, I tell her, "Wait, I'm actually not ready." She laughs again and says she knows.

"When is this going to be over?" I ask her.

"It has just started," she replies.

I tell her I don't understand what is going on with me right now, and she says that change is hard and that part of me wants to remain the same. And that is the part of me that is fighting the experience in different ways, the part that does not want to change. She adds there is no need to judge this part of me, but it can be good to recognize it.

I am now slowly but clearly writhing on the bed. Again, I ask her what is happening. She tells me I have a very strong ego or set of psychological defenses and that is the part of me asking all the questions.

She offers the booster dose. I decide I didn't come today to go halfway and take it.

MDMA is not a classic psychedelic in that it is not a hallucinogen. There are no crazy shapes or strange colors. I actually feel very lucid, awake, and alert. Mostly, I feel calm and light. It feels like I can breathe for the first time, that a heavy vest has finally been lifted off my shoulders. My mind is quiet.

Before the session, I didn't know I had a loud voice in my head, but I quickly recognize that not only do I have one, but it is bone-crushingly loud. And without such a deafening voice, it feels like I am seeing the world in a whole new way.

But as I am feeling a euphoric sense of peace, another part of me is sad. Because it is only when this ever-present chattering voice in my head has dimmed that I can see how anxious and unhappy I am when I am not on this drug. And how much this constant anxiety has driven my life so far.

As sad as I am feeling, however, there also comes an empathy for myself that I don't ever remember feeling before. Yes, I am anxious in a way I haven't seen, but it also feels—at least in this moment—that I have done the best I could.

Slow tears start coming out of me for the first time in a long time.

I am deep enough in my own thoughts and feelings that I don't notice Rachel is now sitting inches away from me until her dog starts making noise at her feet. I tell her I am not sure why I am crying, and she says it doesn't really matter why. That our intellect often uses thinking as a distraction from the painful emotions inside us that we don't want to feel.

She asks if she can hold my hand and I say yes. She reminds me that if I want to, to say the word "allow" out loud. I do, and she clenches my hand and says that is great.

I go deeper, and the next time I catch my breath, I am not crying anymore, and Rachel is not touching me. I take my mask off for a second and look around. She is back in her chair reading a book. We make eye contact.

"Am I okay?"

"You're more than okay," she tells me. "From my perspective, you're doing very well today."

I lie there with my mask off, staring into space. She interrupts me and says it is better to have the mask on, that it helps me stay internal in my feelings, instead of concentrating on external things like her bookshelf. When I put the mask back on, I feel high to the point where I am not sure I could get up.

But I don't want to get up. This experience is much stronger and more introspective than the times I did molly in college. My pelvis is not fine, but my whole body feels so warm, so relaxed, that right now, at least, the state of my pelvis almost doesn't matter to me.

But as my mind goes there for the first time, a wave of fear hits in a way I can't ever remember feeling sober. I see how terrified I am that I will never feel normal again, that I will always remain as alone and isolated as I am now. That one of the things I want most is a deeper sense of connection to others. And how much of the anger I had at the doctors was actually a deep sense of sadness that not only were they not helpful, but most of them did not seem to care.

Rachel asks if I want her to come over there, and I realize I must be showing signs of agitation. I mumble no, even though a part of me very much wants her to come over.

My whole body is shaking now, not just my legs. And just like that, as quickly as it came on, the feelings of fear are gone. I can tell they have not been resolved, but I feel light again now, like some part of me has decided that is enough fear for today.

The rest of the session is a bit of a blur. It is so jarring that both my body and brain spend much of the rest of the time adjusting. My mind is running fast, but at the same time my thoughts are much clearer, like all the bullshit has been stripped away.

As the session goes on, I home in on myself and my family without realizing it. It feels like I am seeing both me and them for how we really are, not the idealized way I want us all to be. I see times when my parents were not there for me as a kid. Times when we didn't connect emotionally and I felt hurt, or instances when I complained about things and they turned it back on me. I have not thought about any of this in a long time. Now I am seeing these moments again, but this time with more clarity, almost from a witness perspective.

I realize I did not see it as a kid the way I am seeing it now not because it was false but because it was painful. But here, lying down with a mask on, these memories coming up feel light in a way I can handle them.

While there is some sadness surfacing, there is more anger. I realize that even aside from anything to do with me, my parents as individuals are far from flawless. The spotlight hovers on them, on us, for a long time.

Before the session, I would have echoed my parents' implicit and occasionally explicit narrative that while they may not have been perfect, they were pretty good. And that while my childhood may not have been amazing, it was fine. I decide on MDMA that I am no longer sure these narratives are correct.

It isn't until Rachel checks in that I realize I haven't said anything for a while. I tell her it feels like it has been an hour since we started. She says it has been almost four hours. I tell her I want more medicine now, and she says that is a sign the MDMA is wearing off and that I can't have any more medicine today, but I can do it again in a month or two if I want. I tell her I just want this feeling of lightness to last forever. She laughs and says she understands. My legs continue to shake gently as they have the entire time.

As the session is winding down, I have what feels like a vision of the future rather than the past. I see myself trudging in New York City in the cold, and how miserable I have been. I realize that this session today was the last thing I needed to do in the city, and now it is time to go. And then I see myself in the Texas sun, eating tacos from a food truck I have been to before in Austin.

"I need to move to Austin as soon as I can," I hear myself saying out loud. "I'll be able to find people who can help me there."

"That sounds like a good idea to me," Rachel says. "For now, it is time to take the mask off and start reintegrating."

I hesitate for a second, hoping that, if I keep the mask on, the euphoria will return. Eventually I accept that it won't.

The second I take the mask off, it's like flipping a switch. My brain hurts. Life sucks, and I feel a total emptiness come over me. I put both hands on the sides of my forehead and sigh deeply.

For the first time all day, Rachel frowns. She hands me a bunch of supplements to take and hustles to get me some food. My jaw is still clamping down, and I can tell it will be very sore tomorrow. I am grimacing and still breathing heavily, Rachel's intense gaze staring right back at me.

Even as it is happening, I know I am not in life-threatening danger, but my head is pounding so hard I can't think about anything else. It is a similar sensation but levels past the worst alcohol hangover I've ever had.

As I get some food in me and the supplements kick in, the headache dims, and I start talking to Rachel about what it was like in there. I am full of things to say now; it feels like a drunk openness, except my thoughts are totally lucid.

Rachel says I will probably be more "open" for the next couple of days and maybe longer as my psyche reorganizes.

"Why did it feel so different today than when I did this at a concert?" I ask.

She says the biggest reasons are mindset and setting. The mask, the relaxed environment, and the background music play a role. There also seems to be something about setting an intention, that someone knows going in that they are initiating their healing journey in a safe space that helps them do so. And I did take plenty of MDMA today, and unlike in party settings, she made sure it was pure.

I ask her what happened at the end there. She says the ego has similarities to a muscle and that just like a muscle, it can hurt when a very tight muscle that is not used to being stretched snaps back. But the comedown is not usually as rough as what happened to me.

As she hands me more supplements to take over the next couple of days, I frown and realize there are parts of the session I think I have forgotten. She says this is common for the first session, that the brain adjusts over time and things start to slow down. She says it is also possible I have "dissociated" and not remembered some things because they were too hard for my brain to handle.

I am frustrated, but she says it is nothing to be mad about, that she herself has dissociated before. "The ego knows what you are ready to handle. Things from today will keep coming back over time, sometimes in strange ways or in future sessions."

When Rachel goes into the other room, I start putting on my shoes and am halfway out the door when she comes back. She looks at me and asks where I am going. I tell her I don't want to take any more of her time and am grateful for the experience. She says my eyes look like saucers and she is not sure I am ready to be walking out the door right now. As she is talking, I see there is a part of me that wants to pretend today didn't happen, and bolting out the door very much fits with that desire. I hate feeling vulnerable, and lying down on this bed, I am not feeling so in control right now.

I lie back down. Rachel says that talk therapy is a good way to start integrating what has come up today and recommends a man named Bruce. She adds that people who try to go right back on with their lives after medicine tend not to get as much out of the experience—and in some cases even get worse because they don't know how to deal with what has come up. She encourages me not to make any big decisions in haste, that it is often better to sit and try to process for a bit before taking action or talking to a bunch of people about it.

Walking out, my pelvis still feels exactly the same. But on the subway back, I feel a mixture of shock and elation that I experienced a whole new way of looking at the world today.

When I get home, I am both exhausted and wired, mind still reeling, replaying the session in my head. I sleep horribly that night, but I wake up several times to myself saying the word "wow" out loud.

# My Earliest Years

had never considered my childhood much, not because it was good or bad but because I thought it was unremarkable.

I was born on November 22, 1993, in the Chicago suburbs as an only child. Both of my parents worked full time when I was growing up My mom, in particular, was a rising star and on the corporate CEO track.

So while my parents were home at night and on weekends to take care of me, I spent much of my early years with babysitters at our house. I have fond memories of playing with toys, watching movies, or reading with them. One of them even invited some of her friends over, and the four of us were having a dance party in the living room when my mom got home from work. I felt loved by most of these women, although much later I came to realize that one of them definitely did not love me.

My favorite thing to do when I was growing up was spending time with my mom. Some of it was because she was not around that often, but I also felt like she got me best.

Sometimes on weekends, the two of us walked into our small town, got ice cream, and sat near the train tracks for a while. My mom would grab a schedule, and together we'd figure out where each train was going while watching them whiz by toward Chicago. I loved it.

It helped that I could do no wrong with my mom—she seemed to think I was the greatest, and she almost never got mad at me.

Except when I got upset first, especially if it had anything to do with her.

Once, we were running late to a movie, and when we got there all the showings for the night were sold out. I started crying. My mom got frustrated. Couldn't I see she was doing her best, that she was trying her hardest? She told me she wouldn't take me to the movies anymore if I was going to get upset.

As a little kid, I cried all the time. I cried when my trains couldn't connect together the way I wanted. I cried when someone died in the movie I was watching. I often even cried when I was happy.

Sometimes when I got sad, my mom seemed unsure what to do and would give her version of the silent treatment while I steadied myself. Other times she would tell me that my crying was making her feel bad in a way that made me feel like I needed to stop. I loved my mom the most and felt guilty whenever she got mad at me. I also wanted her to love me, so over time, I learned that showing any negative emotion around her was my fault and something to hide.

My parents separated in 1997. My dad moved into a rental one town over. I remember his long, twisted driveway and that not having all my things in one place felt disorienting.

Growing up, my dad could make me laugh, and he always seemed to know the answers when I asked him questions about how the world worked. But he was also a yeller in a way that sometimes made me sad. With him, I felt like I was doing something wrong as often as I was doing something right.

He did not always seem interested in my hobbies, like my trains, or how I felt about things.

But from my earliest years, we both loved to read and everything about sports. I have fond memories of going to see the Michael Jordan Bulls with him in Chicago and watching the games at his house while we ate pizza.

He enrolled me in sports camps as early as he could. I loved to compete and sobbed every time I lost.

I struggled to communicate with other four- and five-year-olds. Instead of paying me compliments, they mostly just grunted and picked their boogers. Between my indifference to them and my mom preferring to work rather than drink coffee or wine with the other suburban moms, I spent more time around adults than other kids when I was little.

The highlights of my early childhood were the times my mom took me with her on work trips. I had my own Southwest pass and would bring all my trains in a duffel bag. In the mornings, my mom would park me in an empty conference room near her office. Her coworkers would often come visit me in there, even helping me build my sets. Sometimes I would notice they were not setting up the trains, each of whom I had named, correctly, so I would show them exactly how I wanted them.

"What do you do every day?" I asked my train-set assistants. "Where are you from?"

It never occurred to me that I could not ask these questions or that I should be intimidated by adults.

They frequently paid me compliments around my precociousness, which I loved and made me want to spend even more time around them.

My mom's assistant was tasked with keeping an eye on me and would often take me out for lunch as I waved to everyone I passed. Whenever I visited, I felt like the king of the office.

I took stuffed animals like Winnie the Pooh with me everywhere, and at nights, whether I was home or on the road, I would tuck her in right next to me in bed and wished her goodnight.

In 1999, when I was five years old, my parents got back together. We moved as a family to Connecticut for my mom's job in New York City. This was the peak of the internet boom, and my mom was right in the middle of it. When she was not traveling, she took the train into the city before I got up in the morning and usually got home after I went to bed.

I started going to kindergarten, and there weren't many office visits anymore. I would often be at home with just my dad and our golden retriever, Jackson, in the evenings and sometimes on weekends.

After eighteen months of this, my mom decided to leave the Northeast for more space and a better commute. Just as we were getting ready to move, she found out she was pregnant with my brother. We moved to northern Virginia, about forty-five minutes outside of Washington, DC, in August of 2000, just in time for me to start first grade.

# Dissociating

I spend the days after my first session in a daze, walking around New York City, mind whirling, reviewing it all in my head.

Things feel louder in the city now, in an environment that suddenly seems so rough and unnatural. I begin making definitive plans to move to Austin.

I don't know anyone who has done MDMA therapeutically and have no idea what is normal in the aftermath. A week after the session, I talk with Rachel on the phone to try to integrate the experience. She says some anxiety afterward is common. But when I tell her my legs are still shaking from time to time, she is concerned and advises it could be a good idea to wait longer than usual to do another session and see what comes up.

I meet with Bruce, the therapist Rachel recommended, every week over Zoom. He is not what I envisioned. He is in his mid-fifties, served in the military, and spent a decade as a tradesman before becoming a therapist. I can tell from the clothes he wears, the state of his office, and how much he charges per session that he has blue-collar sensibilities. But he matches the gruff exterior with a softer side. Both his parents died at a young age, so he bounced around with relatives and didn't have two nickels to rub together growing up. He was not in a good place in his twenties, but therapy helped him get his life together, and that is why he decided to become a therapist.

But over time he has grown a bit disillusioned with talk therapy. In his view, it is all intellectual and can only go so far on its own. Five years ago, another therapist turned him onto doing psychedelics therapeutically. He says these compounds revitalized him after some personal and professional stagnation. He likes working with patients who are doing both psychedelics and talk therapy because he believes that together they lead to deeper healing.

Before psychedelics, I felt like I was spinning my wheels and not getting anywhere in therapy. But now I find myself with all sorts of things to say.

Bruce specializes in family systems, and we spend much of the early sessions discussing my family. In one session, I blast my parents from start to finish in a way that surprises me as it bubbles over. Bruce lets me talk uninterrupted, listening, saying it is good at the beginning just to get these feelings out and we can work through them later on. The next session, he says a good first step is to try to appreciate what my family did give me and that everyone's family gave them something, even if just genetically. But he adds that no family is perfect and it can be good to identify where my family may have fallen short because those are the things to work on as an adult.

He observes that I almost always give intellectual answers, "I think" versus "I feel," and that even in talk therapy it is good practice to try to start getting in touch with these deeper emotions. He says the intellect is just a part of a whole person and that intelligence has nothing to do with emotional work or healing—and if anything can be a hindrance because smart people have a tendency to overanalyze and talk themselves into circles. He notes that people who are hyper intellectual at the expense of the emotional are often that way from some sort of early wounding.

Bruce pushes me at times, but I always feel like he is on my side. I decide early on that I like him.

But even with Bruce, I am having a hard time. The session didn't feel that rough as it was happening, but the further I get away from it, the worse things seem to be getting. Before MDMA, I may have been miserable, but I felt very in control of myself and my emotions. I do not feel as in control now. I often wake up nervous and jittery without any reason. I have occasional moments where I feel as calm as I can ever remember feeling. But there are many more times when I get sad or anxious, particularly around my body, in ways that scare me.

Before the session, my pelvis was a constant concern, but one that I tried not to dwell on except when I was seeing specialists. It was too panic-inducing to think about all the time. In the weeks after the session, it begins to sink in both that my pelvis has not improved at all and I still have no idea what to do about it.

I become even more obsessive about how to fix it, constantly googling, searching for ideas, finding more doctors, this time focused on healing chronic pain. One of them wants to insert an electrical nerve stimulator into my pelvis as some sort of pain relief therapy. Another mentions ketamine because it is known for resetting pain receptors.

I go home to my parents' house, unsure what to do next.

One night, I forget to turn the oven on. My mom comes home and is annoyed. I scream at her in a way that surprises both of us and then immediately break down and start crying. She looks perplexed and concerned. I begin to believe my pelvis is destined to be like this forever.

I tell some friends I may have some sort of permanent erectile dysfunction. They look at me like I'm crazy and don't know what to say. But it feels true to me. I still have not brought up my MDMA session with anyone but Bruce.

I decide that my pelvis didn't improve when I did MDMA, so it's time to try something else. I am desperate for any sort of quick fix to make the fear go away.

I get it in my head that ketamine can fix my pelvis, can fix me, maybe even within the week. I go into a quasi-religious fervor around it, frantic that I need to do it as soon as possible.

Unlike MDMA, ketamine is legal, so it's easy to find clinics. I decide to do it at home in Virginia because I won't be able to drive afterward and may need someone's help taking care of myself.

After a twenty-minute intake with a doctor on Friday, I sign up for a week's worth of escalating doses of daily ketamine starting the following Monday. Bruce expresses some concern about the ketamine, but he says it is up to me and he believes people pick the right medicine for them. If he had tried to dissuade me, I would not have listened to him.

The first morning, the nurse inserts an IV in my arm and leaves me in the room by myself. I quickly start getting agitated and paranoid. It is more disorienting than scary. No memories are coming up, but I feel disconnected from my body at times, like I am floating outside it.

The nurse checks in periodically, or so I'm told, but I don't really remember this happening. In the afternoon, my mom comes to pick me up from the clinic and visits me in the outpatient room. My IV is still in and I am barely able to recognize her. Later, she tells me, "It looked like your eyes were coming out of your head."

She immediately goes to the doctor and expresses concern. He says the whole week is needed for the protocol to work, and a combination of him and a drugged-out me overrule her, with me telling her, "You just don't understand."

The doctor decides that tomorrow he will give me ketamine combined with escalating doses of Ativan, a benzodiazepine, so I can calm down and "let the ketamine do its thing." I throw up on the way to the car the first afternoon. We have to pull over on the way home for me to throw up again. Ketamine impairs short-term memory, so I don't remember throwing up very well, but my mom does.

I am barely there the rest of the week. The second they start giving me escalating doses of Ativan, I am down for the count. I throw up every day and lose almost ten pounds. I can tell my mom thinks this whole thing is a horrible idea, but I am so desperate I don't care. I do have an almost dreamlike revelation on the last day of the treatment—a voice in my head tells me that something is really not right with me and my body, that I need to go back to MDMA, and not to try any other medicines for a while.

By Friday night I feel more strung out than when I started. The doctor gives me more ketamine and Ativan to take home, but my mom insists I come off everything cold turkey. I am up almost thirty-six hours straight. She and I spend all night Friday and Saturday walking laps around my neighborhood while I try to calm down.

It seems like there is nothing to integrate from the experience because I was so out of it. But something happened in there. Cars seem to be coming at me faster than ever and I am picking up things in my hearing and field of vision in a way I wasn't before.

I make the move to Austin weeks later. Rachel says it will be better for me to find a MDMA guide there and wishes me well. Through the grapevine, I get introduced to Amy, who works in a healing field. On the phone, she has a warm, almost melodic voice that makes me feel comfortable. I tell her I did one MDMA session before in New York and it was a little intense but I handled it okay, that I had a weird experience with ketamine, and that I just moved here.

Amy asks what has brought me to this work, and I say issues with my parents because that is what has been coming up for me since my first session. She says that is perfectly normal. I tell her I am also having pelvic floor problems. She does not sound worried; she has seen that before and thinks it will go away soon. She says it is my choice but I seem like a good candidate for this work. I waver several times about being ready to do MDMA again, but by the end of the call I am firm: I want to do it. She notes that she can hear the conviction in my voice.

She happens to have a spot the following Saturday and no other openings for two months. I have been in Austin for less than a week and don't really know anyone there. I did a bunch of ketamine five weeks ago. I say yes anyway and don't tell anyone but Bruce that I am doing this.

At this point, I have read the book *The Body Keeps the Score* and think I understand trauma better. I now believe everyone holds stress somewhere and I happen to hold mine in my pelvic floor. All I have to do is shake a little bit of anxiety out of my pelvis in this one session, and then it will be fixed and I can move on from this horrible period in my life for good. The person guiding me in these sessions does not matter because we don't talk much anyway.

In contrast to the first session and my experiences with ketamine, I am super anxious this time around. I can hardly think about anything else in the days leading up to the appointment. I spend hours pacing around my new neighborhood, alone both in my thoughts and in real life. The morning of, I am wide awake by 4:00 a.m.

Amy does not yet have her own space to facilitate sessions and had recommended getting a hotel in the area. I awkwardly meet her for the first time in the hotel lobby. From the get-go, everything feels "off," nothing like my first session in New York where everything felt right.

I am shaking in the elevator up to the room, but if Amy had suggested we stop or postpone, I would have brushed her off. I have come too far to cancel.

Amy says I am the eleventh client she has seen by herself, and her youngest. She is confident, cheerful, and everything she says and does indicates she thinks today will be fine. I take the first dose without hesitating and lie down on the bed with my mask on. As Amy starts talking, I begin to panic out of what feels like a mixture of fear and sadness.

And then everything goes dark.

MDMA takes about thirty to forty-five minutes to start having effects, but I black out before that in the same way someone would brace themselves for a car crash they know is coming. I don't remember taking the booster dose, but Amy tells me later that when she held it out in her hand, I grabbed it.

When I come to, it feels like it has been a long time, maybe several hours. I can tell I have lost whatever just happened. I am violently shaking, not just my legs this time but my whole body—and not in slow motion but very fast, flailing all over the bed like I am being dragged by an ocean current in a way I can't stop.

As I reorient, I realize I am making sound and that I have probably been making sounds this entire time. I don't recognize the noises coming out of me, though. It is not like any sound I have ever made before. It is not words, screams, or even crying. It is similar to moans, like a wounded animal whimpering out its last breaths. It sounds inhuman.

My mask is still on. And even though I have regained consciousness, my brain feels blank, like it is being blocked by a brick wall. As one part of me is making these horrible sounds, another part feels like it is observing me make them from somewhere outside of me.

And then suddenly, I stop making sounds. My body shaking slows down. The feeling that I am seeing outside of myself goes away, and the veil over my brain lifts.

I regain the ability to talk. The peak of the session feels over. All sorts of thoughts are coming up now. The second I have enough breath, I start speaking nonstop. I am also gasping for air like I have just sprinted up a mountain. The energy in the room feels very different.

"Amy, what happened?" I ask over several heaving breaths. "I don't remember anything."

Amy hesitates, and when she does speak, her tone is far less upbeat than before. "You were shaking for almost two hours, making some really tough sounds...I'm not sure you want to remember that."

I can't stop talking in between gasps. It feels like I am saying all these profound things, but later I will see that I am talking so much as a distraction to try to deflect what just happened, that my rambling stream of consciousness makes it impossible to actually think about anything.

I talk about my parents, my friends, the hotel—everything but me and whatever just happened today. I speculate several times that my mom was sexually abused as a child.

I am still terrified and at times ask Amy to help me. Sometimes she touches my foot, and sometimes she does not give any indication she is there at all, which leaves me feeling alone.

One time I say something and get no response, and I realize she has gone to the bathroom. When she comes back, I get mad and tell her I don't like when people abandon me. She gets upset and says she is hurt. After that, I start repeating "I am sorry" over and over again.

She seems to have trouble understanding what I'm saying with my mouthguard in and with how heavily I'm breathing. I feel fear from her, like this is not what she was expecting at all today. And several times I can hear and feel that fear turn into judgment of me, my family, and my suffering.

Then Amy says it is time to start coming out of it now. I am still having trouble breathing, and my body is still shaking. I was so immersed that it never occurred to me I could take off the mask or get up. When I finally take off the mask, Amy's face looks white like she has just seen a ghost.

After a couple of minutes, I am still panting and otherwise struggling, lying down on the bed, my shirt off from how heavily I've been sweating. Amy tells me in a quivering voice to go take a shower. I stumble to the bathroom. I spend minutes trying to figure out how to turn the shower on, still very high, my chest hurting from all the contractions, feeling like I just got hit by a bus.

When I lie back down, she hands me some food and some pot gummies to take. My stomach is empty, and the pot is strong. My breathing slows, although I feel even more out of it after that.

She asks me if I have anything I want to say about today, and I mumble no. She says that is the most she has ever seen anyone shake and she is concerned. She mentions several times that I need energy work. I have no idea what this means and do not ask.

She also names an SSRI she has recently gone on, and while she says it is my choice, she strongly recommends I go on it as well.

It does not feel like the time to be discussing SSRIs or the future. I am still very much struggling to get through right now, panicked, disoriented, judging myself for what happened today. It feels like a lecture, like I have done something wrong—or worse, that something really is wrong with me.

Amy says she is sorry for my suffering and seems like she means it. But it feels like pity more than empathy. She tells me I am eventually going to be okay, but she doesn't say it with much conviction.

I am now high on weed and not capable of having a full-fledged conversation. She says she is going home to go cook dinner and strongly encourages me to spend the night here. It feels strange to receive the lecture she just gave right before she leaves me alone for the evening.

I barely get up to give her a half-hearted hug. I don't move much the rest of the night, only sending a short response to her check-in text to tell her I am okay.

This brutal day in the hotel is my wake-up call that something is deeply wrong here—and whatever it is, I'm not going to fix it overnight or by myself.

# The Dream

When I call the Uber the next morning, I can tell I'm in trouble. My brain feels scrambled, and while I'm still piecing everything together, I know that whatever happened yesterday was not good.

The first couple of hours are okay. I go for a walk and lie down to try to get some rest. And then I start having trouble breathing, alone in my apartment in the middle of the afternoon. I am gasping for air again, like yesterday, involuntarily. I don't know what I am panicking about, just that I feel anxious in a way I have never felt before.

My heart feels like it is beating out of my chest. The struggle to breathe lasts a couple of minutes, but it feels much longer.

I have no idea what to do. It feels like I have blown a fuse somehow in the session.

I have a hard time breathing again when I try to go to bed that night, waiting it out for minutes as the anxiety slowly dissipates and my breathing steadies.

The next couple of days are rough. I wake up in the morning after a horrible night's sleep, huffing and puffing like I am in the middle of a marathon. I pace outside for hours trying to calm down. It is hard to work because I am too on edge to sit. I don't know what to do or who to call. I talk to Bruce a couple of times on the phone, but he is far away. I am too embarrassed to reach out to anyone else.

I am having such a difficult time trying to wind down in the evening that I try some more of the pot Amy gave me. It only makes things worse.

At one point, I think I might be in enough danger to consider going to an urgent care facility, but I don't, mostly because I don't want to explain what brought me there or feel even more like something is wrong with me.

I'm not even sure what I am anxious about. It feels more to do with my nervous system than with my thoughts. But it seems dangerous and unsustainable.

More than once, I think, *What have I done here?*

Later in the week, I have yet another scheduled doctor's appointment with a renowned men's sexual health specialist. It has been on the calendar for months, and I have to fly back to New York City for it. It never occurred to me when I scheduled my psychedelic session that flying to see this doctor five days later would be an issue.

Even though I am a mess, I decide to go to New York anyway. I text my mom that I am having trouble, and she decides to meet me there. I am shaking coming off the airplane. When I arrive at the hotel, my mom takes one look at me and says we need to go for a walk somewhere.

It takes me forever to fall asleep.

That night, I have the most vivid dream I have ever had in my life. I am an adult, but in it I am getting raped in the piano room of my childhood home.

I wake up in a panic, alone in a New York hotel room, and

the realization forms in my head that my elementary school music teacher and piano tutor, Mr. Bishop, raped me at least several times in my home and in his car on the way to the lessons. I have not seen or communicated with him since I left elementary school fifteen years ago.

The whole thing feels surreal, and there are no distinct memories associated with it, but when I wake up that morning, it comes with an alarm that rocks me.

*How did this all happen?* I wonder. *Where is he now?* I am frantically googling his name when my mom walks in and says we are running late to the doctor. I text Bruce and tell him I think my music teacher raped me when I was a kid.

I meet with the doctor's assistant, who asks me all the same questions everyone has been asking me for years. When did my pelvic floor problems start? Have I tried pelvic floor physical therapy? Have I tried Viagra? I am stuttering, rambling, and feeling very off kilter.

He is midsentence when I blurt out, "I have been doing psychedelics to try to get my pelvis fixed, and I think I was raped as kid by my piano teacher in his car and at my house."

The PA's eyes go wide. After an awkward silence, he tells me that he is going to get the doctor now. It feels so strange to say this out loud, like I must be dreaming because I can't believe it just came out of my mouth.

After what feels like an eternity, the doctor comes in. The first thing he says is that I am going to be okay. "Your pelvic floor situation is unusual. I was scrolling through your file this morning and had no idea what I was going to tell you, but this certainly clears things up."

He encourages me to tell my parents, telling me that it was a different era and even that one of his teachers drove students home all the time, although he doesn't think he was a rapist. He says I can still live a good life, but this will probably be the low point. He strongly encourages me to check myself in somewhere if things get tough. He is pleased I am seeing a therapist and says I am crying out to be medicated, so he writes me a prescription for an SSRI. We talk for twenty minutes, and he pats me on the shoulder goodbye. The whole conversation feels like I am talking about someone else.

My mom is waiting as I walk out of his office. We walk around Central Park, and I am just about to tell her I was raped when something stops me. I am suddenly not so sure anymore; it is like a window that was wide open this morning has slammed shut. I know that once I tell her, I won't be able to take it back.

*Maybe I'm just reaching for a neat explanation for all my issues*, I think. I've been a mess since the session. Maybe I'm going crazy here.

There are no memories coming back. I can't see it at all.

But the thing I keep coming back to the most is if he was really raping kids that long ago, why hasn't he been caught by now? I see on Google that he has recently switched elementary schools but is still employed in the same county where I grew up and my family still lives.

Instead of telling my mom, I decide to call Amy. I am freaked out and cut right to the chase. "Did I ever say anything about being sexually abused?" I ask.

"You said multiple times that you thought your mom had been abused—"

"No, no," I interrupt. "Not my mom. *Me.*"

"I don't remember anything like that," she says.

There's an awkward silence.

"I have to go," I say.

That call, lasting less than sixty seconds, is the last time we speak. I delete her number from my phone in much the same way I am trying to erase the past week from my mind.

In the midst of all this, Bruce texts that he is here for me if I want to talk. I write him a rambling text that I am embarrassed, I am reaching to find an explanation for all my issues, and I am having a rough week. He says it is all part of the healing process and he will be here if I need him.

Instead of flying back to Austin, my mom says she thinks it would be a good idea for me to go back to Virginia with her for a bit. When I insist on heading back a couple of days later, she announces that she will be coming with me. She says it's to keep helping me move in, but I can tell it is really because she is concerned about my mental state.

We get back on July 4, and the fireworks start going off as I am trying to sleep. I'm so wired that they sound like gun shots, my whole body cowering each time one goes off even after I know they are coming.

After a couple of days, I blow up at my mom and tell her I need space right now. She seems mystified about what is going on with me. I've sent her several media articles about psychedelics healing trauma and at one point say I think I had a rougher childhood than I'd thought, which offends her.

We have talked around but not directly about my own usage. She doesn't seem to get it and at one point asks why I am doing them. She is justifiably concerned that I seem to be getting worse.

She flies back to Virginia, and we barely communicate over the next several months.

The summer alone in Austin is horrible. All the fears that the first session brought up around my pelvis and my body as a whole are still there but much worse now. They are running loops of catastrophizing thoughts that seem to have no resolution that I start to call "doom loops." Once I start thinking these thoughts, I have a hard time stopping; they feel almost addicting.

It is like a stereo has been turned on full blast with the intensity of my thoughts, my fears, as well as what I am picking up on outside of me. I have anxiety attacks regularly and occasionally have trouble breathing to the point where I can feel them coming on. Sometimes I go for walks out in the heat to try to calm down.

I feel a combination of tired but wired all the time. One time while driving, I am on a two-lane road, and the car in the other lane feels like it is coming right at me. I am so freaked out I have to pull over to try to calm down.

I wake up several days convinced—with no evidence—that I am about to be fired from my job.

I go to a doctor, certain my minor hip surgery was botched and that my hips are permanently damaged. He can't even tell I had the surgery.

I also start to feel an existential dread. I have never thought about dying much, but now I fear that not only will I die one day, but that day could be very soon.

I realize I didn't know what true anxiety was until I started doing MDMA.

I am not sure what to do. There doesn't seem to be a playbook about how to manage this kind of anxiety, other than to go on drugs.

I try an SSRI for a couple of days, and while I know it is not nearly long enough, I already don't like how it is making me feel physically. I also know I don't want to be on one forever, and I can't go on it if I want to keep doing psychedelics.

Bruce thinks microdosing psilocybin mushrooms is a much better fit for me. He puts me in touch with someone who sends me bags of 0.1 g psilocybin teas and capsules. I start microdosing every couple of days and notice I feel a little calmer but also a little sadder about my family and childhood on days that I do.

At times when I am really struggling with anxiety, I tell Bruce that I feel messed up and that everyone including Amy judges me.

Bruce says there is nothing wrong with me and that I am just going through a rough period right now. In regard to Amy, he tells me that there are a lot of people starting to facilitate medicine work, some of whom have not always done their own work and can get overwhelmed by the experience. He adds that when people become more awake and in touch with their emotions after being disso-ciated for a long time, things can and often do get worse before they get better because all the emotions they pushed down start coming back up.

But he believes in me, reminding me that I showed almost no emotion and was totally closed off when we first met, and since then he has already seen progress. He also had a rough time when he first started doing medicine, but now he feels better than he ever felt before. He encourages me to write a letter to my mom expressing my grievances from my childhood—but strongly discourages me from sending it.

Part of healing, he tells me, is learning how to give yourself what you didn't get as a child, and that can start with embracing healthier habits and self-care techniques. He recommends protein-heavy meals, journaling, and spending as much time in nature as possible, particularly standing with bare feet, a technique he says is called grounding. Neither one of us ever mention the text I sent about Mr. Bishop.

Even with how bad things are, I also feel a tiny amount of excitement. The MDMA experience was so intense I could see it healing my pelvis in a way I never really could with any other modality. Despite all the challenges, I realize pretty quickly I want to do more MDMA at some point.

I am still having all the same pelvic problems. But even with the constant worries about my pelvis, I don't schedule any more doctor's appointments and mostly stop reading about pelvic floor disorders. I start reading books about childhood trauma instead.

All the memories coming back about Mr. Bishop are positive: us laughing at the piano together. Him being super nice to me in music class.

Even though I am a little cynical, it doesn't fit with my worldview that he could still be at a school twenty years after I took piano lessons with him if he was also a child molester. Someone would have done something. I would have said something. People get caught for this sort of thing, I decide at one point.

But I can't seem to put that one back in the box. Why would I just randomly come up with a teacher raping me, especially with my years of horrible pelvic problems? I know enough about trauma to understand how bad childhood sexual abuse is. So there is never any thought he could have raped me but it was not a big deal. Nor is there any thought it could have been someone else. Either he did it, or I am being paranoid, trying to come up with an all-encompassing explanation of my issues.

I Google him on a weekly basis. The only information available is an article introducing him at his new school as someone who likes to take his dogs for walks with his partner, along with a small photo. He has no social media. I don't know how to get more certainty one way or the other. It doesn't seem like a good idea to contact him out of the blue and ask if he raped me. It feels weird to ask anyone else, too, especially my parents.

I find two memories come back as I'm waking up in the morning that feel incomplete in the way other memories of him do not.

First, there is a loud banging on the door that I know is for piano lessons, that I keep hearing in my head, except I am not moving to answer it. I am just standing there as it gets louder and louder.

And another time, I am getting out of his car at my bus stop at the top of my hill. I know he has driven me home a number of times, but it was always to my house. Why would he drop me off at the top of the hill instead?

I journal about this regularly, trying to get more clarity. Several times I wake up convinced he raped me, but by lunch I have doubts, and by dinner I have talked myself out of it.

I notice on days when I microdose, I seem to have more concerns about it. I go back and forth this entire anxiety-filled summer. I vow to figure it out once and for all in my next MDMA session.

My body is still a mess; my neck, hips, shoulders, glutes, and pelvis are all tight. I am referred to a new pelvic floor therapist, someone who apparently takes a more holistic approach.

When I arrive for the first session, she stands behind me to do a quick read. Within ninety seconds, she announces, "Something is off with your field."

"Uh, what do you mean *my field*?"

"Your energy field," she replies, either missing or ignoring my skepticism. "Your neck and shoulders are very far forward. Your psoas is tight, and your pelvis is out of alignment. Do you have trauma?"

"No, I don't think so," I reply because I don't have much trauma, just some anxiety.

All she says is, "Hmmm," and then we get to work.

It is very different than any physical therapy I have ever done before. It is compound full-body movements, things like Pilates and yoga rather than isolated stretches. My balance is so bad I struggle to say upright at times. I can't raise either arm over my head without my shoulders clicking out of place, like they are frozen in certain spots. I quickly realize all my breathing is coming from my chest and feel exhausted.

We also do craniosacral massage, in which she applies pressure to the back of my neck. After a couple of minutes of this, I feel as relaxed as I have in years. For a second, I feel calm—light even.

But things change when we do pelvic floor work. I have done hundreds of pelvic floor therapy sessions and never felt anything beyond physical pain. My pelvis seemed disconnected, almost as though it wasn't there. It still feels that way, but when she goes into my pelvis this time, I also feel a deep, nonspecific fear that I have never felt before. My legs start slowly but visibly shaking.

At the end of the session, she says I really shied away from touch on the table and asks me point blank if I was sexually abused. Maybe a few doctors have asked me this before, but not many. Even when they did, it felt like they were checking off a box.

When she asks me now, it is like I am hearing the question for the first time in much the same way I heard Tucker for the first time.

"No," I say again.

"Hmmm," she again replies.

Every session, she massages my neck, my shoulders, my glutes, or my psoas, and I always feel a little calmer and looser when I leave. But my range of motion is still restricted almost everywhere. After a day or two, all the muscle tension seems to revert back in a way that makes me feel like nothing is sticking and that something deeper is going on.

Even so, I keep seeing her. Lying down on her table is the only thing that is able to relax me all summer.

# First Grade

walked into my crowded public elementary school with a backpack the size of my head, Velcro shoes, and a bowl cut. I knew no one.

I lived in an idyllic suburb, full of woods and parks, wealthy and far enough away from DC where crime was more like an HOA dispute.

There were almost thirty of us in my first-grade class with just one teacher. She was fair and engaged but seemed strict to six-year-old me.

From the second we finished reciting the Pledge of Allegiance, it seemed like someone—usually a boy—was hitting, yelling, or touching inappropriately. She shouted at them to stop because when she spoke normally, no one listened. Whenever she yelled, I felt like it was my fault. Sometimes she had everyone put their heads down in silence to try to calm us down, but it made me feel like I was in trouble. I rarely got in any sort of trouble and cried every time I did.

We spent plenty of time during the day transitioning between activities. Getting everyone to stand in line, not touching each other, in near silence, to go somewhere like art or music was an orchestration.

It was all so different, so disorienting, so much worse than hanging out with the adults in my mom's office or even half-day kindergarten. The days felt so long.

I hated that I now had to ask whenever I needed to go the bathroom. Or when I was enjoying the book I was reading or the writing I was doing, I had to switch activities to something else. Or why when I raised my hand in class to answer her question, she often ignored me and called on someone whose hand was not up.

I knew all sorts of facts and had many thoughts, which I communicated to anyone who would listen. I asked all my teachers questions, like why they decided to become a teacher or why we were doing this activity and not that activity. Most of them did not seem interested in engaging, and one of them said she did not have time to explain it to me.

My outfit of a collared shirt and short shorts, with the occasional sports jersey mixed in, was not blowing my peers away. I tried to share food as a way to make friends and was told this was an allergy concern. Once, I brought a light-up globe to school that spoke all the world capitals. I was excited about it and said anyone who wanted to could try it. It was not the hit I expected and instead became a source of class-wide derision.

Other first graders were a code I could not crack. I would ask them how their day was going or use words I had just learned in a book to little response. At times it felt like they were speaking a different language. It didn't help that sometimes I told them to be quiet and do what the teacher said so we didn't all get yelled at. They called me a tattletale, teacher's pet, and a know-it-all.

I cried often, which led to bullying. Even the other six-year-old boys could tell I was wired differently.

I spent that year focused on solo pursuits. I learned to memorize the presidents backward and forward or the Washington football team's fifty-three-man roster.

There were no boys in my neighborhood, and the houses were far apart on large lots. So while I did organized athletics, I rarely played outside. I spent most of my free time on nights and weekends watching sports or movies or playing with toys by myself.

I walked the quarter mile home, down the hill from the bus stop, alone, usually upset, sometimes crying. When I got home, I often complained to my dad that I did not like school. He didn't seem concerned; sometimes I felt like he had decided what he was going to say before I had finished speaking. He said plenty of people did not like school at first, but over time I would get used to things and find people like me. Occasionally he told me that doing things you do not want to do is part of life.

My mom was not around that much, but when she was, she told me I was amazing and would be fine. Sometimes I felt like an abstraction, that I would always be two years old and perfect to her.

I rarely felt like I had her full attention. Even on weekends she was often busy doing something around work or her pregnancy. Besides, she did not like it when I got upset, so I did my best to never get upset in front of her.

At one point, my parents talked about sending me somewhere else. I visited other schools, but nothing came of it.

My brother was born at the end of October 2000. I frequently asked my parents why he was there. I never got an answer that made sense to me.

One night that fall, my mom called me into the kitchen. She thought I should be doing more after-school activities besides sports. She suggested piano lessons, saying it would expand my horizons. My school music teacher, Mr. Bishop, had advertised at-home piano lessons in the school newsletter I brought home with me.

I did whatever my mom told me, so piano it was. I already knew Mr. Bishop from music class, and he had always been nice to me.

He showed up at our house one Wednesday afternoon, right after school at 4:30 p.m. Mr. Bishop was tall, thin, and young-looking, with a high-pitched voice. He was clean shaven, with blondish hair almost in a crew cut, and had a large Adam's apple. He wore darker, formal clothes and a strange ring on his middle finger that he often fiddled with at the piano.

He was mild mannered and polite, often telling my mom we had a lovely home.

I learned that he was in his mid-twenties and had recently moved to the area. He said he lived in Washington, DC, but commuted out to the suburbs just for our school. He was doing the lessons to make some extra money before driving home every night. Besides, the piano was his favorite instrument, but he didn't get to teach it much to a whole class.

From the outset, I could tell he knew his way around the piano. He told me I was a quick learner and a talented musician, even though from the beginning I preferred sports and rarely practiced. In between playing songs, we talked in the piano room while my dad was out of earshot, occupying himself in other parts of the house.

Mr. Bishop never seemed too tired to answer my questions about why he became a teacher, even taking the time to discuss movies we both had seen or tell me how smart I was. The only time he seemed hesitant was when I asked him where he was from and about his childhood. He said he was from a small town in the Northeast, and even as a little kid I could tell it was time to change the subject.

He asked me all sorts of questions, too, and I could tell from both his questions and responses that he was listening. Sometimes it was about me, what I did for fun, how I liked school, or even about my mom and dad and what we did together. One lesson, I showed him my globe, and he seemed especially fascinated by it, both of us taking turns clicking on different countries and watching them light up.

He said I was doing great in school music. He even told me, in a way that felt like a secret, that I was his favorite kid in class and that none of his other piano students practiced like I did. He often put his hand on my shoulder as he was using his other hand to point something out on the music sheet. He got me my own metronome so I could do a better job counting the beats. He turned it on every time he came.

When my mom was home, he gushed about me to her after the lessons. He told her what a joy I was to have in class, how mature and advanced I was, especially compared to the other boys.

They became friendly, my mom often asking him questions as she wrote him his check while Mr. Bishop waved at my baby brother from across the room. How did he like the DC area? How was he adjusting to our school? Mr. Bishop had a sense of humor, albeit in a nerdy way, and sometimes the three of us shared a laugh, standing in our kitchen, before I walked him out.

He and my dad did not engage much, as my dad was often reading or on his computer. My golden retriever, Jackson, did not take to him, loudly barking when he arrived and jumping on him every time he entered the kitchen in a way that did not always seem so friendly.

Mr. Bishop never felt like a father figure. He was not into sports, which was far and away my first love. But he engaged me in a way I had come to expect before this not-good first-grade year and in a way that reminded me of the adults in my mom's office. Now I had an audience again.

I trusted him because he was my teacher, an adult, and because he seemed to really like me.

I turned seven years old that November.

# Katrina

A month or so after my session with Amy, I am still struggling. The fast-moving cars, constant catastrophizing about my body, and seemingly random anxiety attacks have been rough.

I am desperate enough that I start thinking about the "energy work" Amy mentioned. Through the grapevine I hear of a shaman named Katrina who claims to do energy work in Austin. In my mind, a "shaman" is synonymous with a quack, but I decide to take a look at her website. It talks about the light energy field, the subconscious, imprints, soul retrieval, and a whole host of other topics I think are mostly if not completely bullshit.

But amid the worst summer of my life, something makes me keep thinking about her. I decide to reach out, writing that I am trying to integrate a psychedelic session that is causing me distress.

We start in chairs, in what she calls "the healing room" of her house. Her big dog, Chester, sits at her knee.

I am assuming she is easygoing, someone who is into horoscope readings and spirit animals.

The things she talks about still don't make much sense to me. But from the outset there is an intensity to her that surprises me and leaves me feeling backfooted and uncomfortable.

She asks lots of questions about why I am there. I find myself getting defensive quickly. She does not agree with my narrative that I don't have much trauma or many things to work on. She says blacking out on MDMA is unusual and a sign my brain could not handle whatever was coming up. Katrina is also perplexed by my pelvic situation. She asks point blank if I can jack off and shit, clearly expecting a detailed response about how it is all going down there.

I tell her all the things I think are wrong with my other family members, that they are the ones with the real anxiety. "Yet," she notes, "*you* are the one sitting in the chair talking to me today."

I tell her I think I just didn't have great parents and have a bit of a genetic predisposition to anxiety. She doesn't tell me flat-out that I am wrong, but she makes it clear she does not agree. I don't find myself "winning" many of our exchanges, which frustrates me.

I go on a tangent about places I have enjoyed traveling, and she says, "That sounds like a nice story, but I think we are here to talk about you today."

Sometimes she repeats what I have said earlier. More than once, I interrupt her to say that she is misinterpreting what I meant. She responds with a smile and says that is why she is feeding it back to me, to make sure she has it right.

Katrina tells me that talk therapy works with the conscious, and that is all well and good, but she tries to go a level deeper to the unconscious, that all humans have an unconscious layer, and that is where things start to get interesting. She also says that running energy while breathing on her table can help people tap into that level, into their deeper feelings and memories, without having to take psychedelics.

Half an hour in, I am surprised when she asks if I want to get on the table and start breathing today.

I respond, "Does this actually work?"

"I think so," she says. "But if you ever get uncomfortable and want to leave, that's okay with me."

I feel like she is issuing me a challenge, that behind her words she is saying, "Take it or leave it."

Even during the breathing, I stall and argue over semantics. But eventually, I experience a headrush and find myself crying about feeling abandoned walking home alone from my bus stop as a child. And that it was hard as a kid because whenever I cried in front of my mom she got upset.

At the end, I look up at the clock and am startled to see we have gone almost two hours. I am exhausted; working with her feels much heavier than talk therapy. But I also feel a little lighter as I am leaving.

She says I have a strong ego and did plenty of deflecting from talking about myself and my emotions, but today was a decent start if I decide I want to come back.

Katrina looks surprised when I show up the following week for another session. She says she didn't think I would return, but as long as I keep showing up, she will do her very best to help me.

We keep talking and breathing. One night early on, deep into the breath work, I tell her I have a paranoia about being sexually abused by my piano teacher.

She says she can't know if I was abused but asks how I feel about him, adding that people who have been abused usually do not like their abusers. There is a long pause before I tell her, "I think he was a nice man."

In that moment, I realize I am not actually so sure and immediately change the subject. Neither of us brings it up again.

After a couple of sessions with Katrina—and as I get further away from the blackout in the hotel—I start to feel a little better. I tell her I want to do another MDMA session and ask if she knows anyone who facilitates medicine. She says that, actually, she sometimes works with her energy clients to guide them on psychedelics. And she would be willing to do a medicine session with me if I am up for it.

There is still a whole language to her that I do not understand, around energy, consciousness, and the ego. And she is very spiritual in a way I am not. But I can quickly tell she can help me, maybe more than anyone else ever has. So even though I find working with her challenging and at times annoying, it never occurs to me not to keep seeing her.

I feel I have met my match in a way, and we schedule an MDMA session.

When I arrive at her house for the session, I am terrified, although I'm still not sure why. I tell her that ever since I have started doing medicine, feelings and memories from my childhood have been coming up that I have not thought about in a long time. I say that I would much rather be getting drunk or watching sports than doing any of this, in a way that feels half joking, half completely serious. And I say that I wouldn't be near any of this stuff if my dick was working the way it's supposed to.

She says it is often things in our past that are constraining us now, and perhaps that is what is going on with my pelvis. "But there is no use worrying or speculating," she adds. "Let's not judge the experience. Just see what comes up. Whatever happened in your past, whatever happens today, Chester and I have you."

As the session begins, my body is already in a defensive crouch.

But as it comes on, I can feel myself relaxing. For the first time on MDMA, I am not shaking—just lying there feeling open, calm, and warm. It feels fun.

I tell Katrina I wish everyone could experience how light I feel right now. Katrina warns me against pushing anyone else to do this. It is up to each person on their own if and when they decide psychedelics are for them. And when someone does this because someone else told them to, it tends not to go well.

Right as she says this, fears start coming up around my body, my pelvis again. It is like my brain is stuck there. Even on medicine, I can't envision a scenario where my pelvic floor problems ever go away.

I sit in silence for a while, trying to focus on it, hoping that I can *will* my pelvis to let go. I feel nothing.

I give up and start asking Katrina questions about herself. At first, she seems discouraging of my digressions, but after a while she starts opening up.

She says she had a tough childhood. As an adult, she was in trauma and got into a scarring marriage. When she started going to shaman school and working on herself, he kept putting her down. And as they divorced, he blamed her for everything, saying that he didn't feel like he could live up to her expectations.

I note that it does not always seem to be the happiest people that turn to healing or psychedelics. She laughs and says most people do not work on themselves unless there is some sort of trigger to do so. For some it can be as simple as seeing someone close to them grow for the better. There are others who need to suffer for a while until they decide they want to change. "Then there are those who won't change no matter how much pain they are in," she says, with a darker laugh this time.

I laugh and say I think I am in the second category, but then I realize how scared I am to change and say so.

She replies that psychedelics do not force you to do anything; they sometimes just help you see things in a different way, and from there it will always be my choice. And some people can start making these changes without doing any medicine at all, whereas others just need a little push at the beginning. The intention is that, over time, the psychedelics are less and less needed. She adds that while she did a bunch of psychedelics when she was younger, she does not do them much anymore, only a couple of times in the past decade or so.

She also says that changing or healing, like anything else, is never perfect or finished. But the initial period when the big stuff comes up is usually the hardest.

I talk about an instance when I was bullied in first grade, and I didn't realize it at the time, but that hurt has stayed with me more than I thought. I hated going to school when I was growing up. For the first time, I feel my legs start shaking a bit as I talk about it.

Katrina tells me that in childhood, the brain is always trying to make sense of why things are happening the way they are, when we think everything that happens to us is because of us, and our fundamental beliefs about ourselves are being formed. And these default patterns from childhood tend to come out as adults in things like relationships or work if they are not examined.

I tell her I have not always been nice to people and mention Ashley in Utah. She says it is important to recognize it, acknowledge it, and accept that these things happened, but at the same time not to beat myself up over it. Self-forgiveness is just as important a part of the healing process as forgiving others.

We keep going and start talking about my mom. "I love my mom," I say, feeling my nose scrunch up. "But sometimes I feel like she let me down."

Katrina asks, "How did she let you down?"

Something starts bubbling up inside me. "She left me with people she shouldn't have."

Emotions well up, and my whole body starts shaking. I keep talking as I shake. "I had a babysitter when I was like four who hit me sometimes," I say, realizing this for the first time as my whole body is convulsing.

As my jaw clenches, I manage to continue, forcing out the words. "Something was off with her. She was…erratic. Some days she gave me all this candy. She had so much energy, and we would read together. It felt like she loved me. But other days she would yell a lot. Sometimes I'd ask a question, and she'd get mad and smack me around for a while. She hit herself too. One day she spent a long time hitting me but mostly hitting herself. And there was another time where she just fell asleep the whole day, and I didn't know what to do. It was just me and her at my house during the week for a while."

"How did that make you feel?" Katrina asks.

"Scared," I reply.

But as I finish my thoughts about her, I abruptly stop shaking. "It wasn't that bad," I tell Katrina.

I add that I am not the easiest person to be friends with and have realized from doing medicine that I have mostly closed myself off for a long time. She says that guardedness usually comes from being hurt, the way it sounds like I was with my babysitter.

As the medicine wears off, I tell her my pelvis is still not working. She asks why I think this is, and I tell her I don't know. It is like that part of my brain is blank, like my body is just disconnected from it. It feels like she wants to ask a follow-up question but says nothing.

When I take off the mask, I decide that I like her and, more importantly, that I trust her, that I think we will keep working together, both for the weekly sessions and with the psychedelics. And that I want to do another medicine session soon, that this one feels incomplete.

As I get up, I realize that I was so immersed in the experience and later my babysitter that I forgot about Mr. Bishop. I take this as a positive. I decide the fact that he did not come up today means nothing happened there. I don't mention his name or bring him up in any way out loud.

I am excited as we get up and go for walk with Chester. On the walk, I tell her that this went much better than any session before it, that it was not so bad, that I am feeling better and starting to make progress.

But she doesn't seem as sure.

# Dickhead

feel a little lighter in the weeks after my session with Katrina, but my pelvis has not improved at all. And at times I am still struggling with bad nonspecific anxiety.

I go visit friends in Nashville for the weekend. I have the worst panic attack I've ever had coming off the airplane. On Saturday, I microdose and later start drinking with them. At one point, I find myself wanting to say out loud that I was sexually abused before the thought quickly dissipates into a pool of other drunken thoughts.

The next week, I head to Katrina's for another session. As I put my mask on and the music starts playing, I tell her I've been looking for this medicine for a long time and have a bad feeling about today but am not sure why. She says that whatever happens, she and Chester will be ready.

As it comes on, I start filibustering again. Except this time, Katrina does not engage with me. Sometimes she says a word or two or grunts, but most of the time my empty words just hang in the air.

I take the booster. I am as high as I will get and still rambling when Katrina interrupts me in a loud and declarative voice. "Alex, does your pelvis have anything to say?"

There is no warning, and my first thought is, *She is not supposed to be initiating questions. That's against the rules.*

But I feel an openness, like truth serum, and something slips out before I can stop it. "I was sexually abused by my piano teacher."

I can feel my own shock before I even finish the sentence, and the words just hang there for a second.

Then my pelvis lights up like a bull's-eye, a dull, deep ache that I feel over and over again, like I am getting raped right then and there.

And then the feeling in my pelvis is gone, replaced by the taste of him in my mouth.

I am so stunned I don't even realize that Katrina has hopped over her chair and is now holding my hand.

"I can feel him and taste him," I tell her.

"Rape can leave all sorts of imprints, even decades later."

I'm trembling.

"Whatever happened, it already happened," Katrina says, squeezing my hand as Chester licks my face. "We are going to get you through this."

I start full-body shaking, to the point where she has to let go of my hand. Then the memories start flooding back. It is not just repressed memories that come back on psychedelics—today it's like pulling long-lost items out of a warehouse, things I haven't looked at in a long time and had mostly forgotten were in there. Except this time, they come back with a different perspective, like I am seeing them in a new way.

The first thing that comes back is the eyes.

I am in the music room with my class, and Mr. Bishop is my teacher later on in elementary school. The rapes have been over for a long time. We are all practicing the recorder. A boy in my class has started playing out of turn. The first time, Mr. Bishop politely asks him to stop. The boy does not. Mr. Bishop is now clearly annoyed but still very much in control and asks the boy again to please stop playing while others are having their turn. The boy keeps going, seeming to almost take pride in antagonizing him. The third time, Mr. Bishop shouts, "Excuse me!" and his eyes narrow into slits for a split second before he calms back down.

There are no other adults in the room. I am not sure any of the other kids noticed. But I had seen those eyes before and for a second see how much fear I felt in that moment deep inside.

*CLICK.* The spotlight changes.

I am watching the Michael Jackson verdict with a friend's family in 2005. His dad announces that if anyone touched his son like that, he would kill him with his bare hands, consequences be damned. I say nothing.

*CLICK.* The image shifts again. I see myself getting into Mr. Bishop's car with the dark-tinted windows and feel fear.

*CLICK.* My mom is announcing in the kitchen while I am in high school that my brother and sister are now taking piano lessons with Mr. Bishop after school in his classroom, that he said to say hi to me. I casually ask her whether they are taking lessons with him together or separately, and when she replies together, part of me relaxes inside.

*CLICK.* A male friend is telling me he was raped as a kid and I respond, "I am sorry to hear that," without much compassion.

*CLICK.* Mr. Bishop and my mom are chatting at my sixth-grade graduation. I watch myself sprint to hug him. Both of them are smiling.

*CLICK.* As my elementary school graduation is winding down in my school gym, Mr. Bishop comes and finds me. He smiles and says he has loved teaching me and wishes me well. We make eye contact and shake hands; it lasts all of thirty seconds. I realize that while we occasionally waved in the school hallways, we never had a one-on-one conversation after he stopped teaching me piano until that handshake. And that handshake is the last time I ever communicate with him.

*CLICK.* I see my mom reading his gushing email apologizing that he can no longer teach me piano, that I will always be one of his favorite students, and I feel how ecstatic I am that he quit.

*CLICK.* I see him fondling me over my shorts at the piano as he tells me what a great job I am doing, neither one of us acknowledging he is touching me. My dad is in the other room.

I am still trembling, my whole body shaking as I start muttering, "Violent motherfucker," and "Butt stuff," out loud, although I still can't tell exactly why I am saying these things.

As the session goes on, it comes out that he has choked me at least once, maybe many more times than that. "I can't see the actual rapes," I say, frustrated. "It's like I'm blocked. I can't go there."

"Visuals come last because they are the hardest," Katrina says. "For now, focus on what you remember and the feelings around it. Everything that needs to will come back over time."

She adds that even from what I brought up today, there will be plenty of things to work on in energy moving forward.

As the medicine begins to wear off, we shift gears and start talking about the future. Katrina encourages me to tell my mom and close friends. She thinks I will be in a "healing crisis" for a while, where things get worse before they get better, and it will be important to have their support.

On the walk around her block, I am still in shock. Sometimes it doesn't seem so bad. But other times it hits me all at once. Several times I have to sit down for a second. One time, I have to hold on to Katrina.

There is a part of me that still wants to put the whole thing back in the box, pretend today did not happen. At one point, I say, "Even people who have been raped a lot don't have their dick stop working for years at a time. I think it was as bad as it gets."

I start quivering in ninety-degree heat, and Katrina gives me a hug. She says it was obvious from the get-go that something was going on with me, that it was probably sexual abuse, and she remembers me talking about Mr. Bishop once in energy, but that I just would not go there.

She tells me that I was as locked in as anyone she had ever worked with, that I was sure there was absolutely nothing wrong with me, even as I continued to show up at her house every week. And she or anyone else can't really go there before I go there. But we have worked together long enough that she felt comfortable trying to take things to the next level today.

"I don't understand how I could not remember this," I say.

"Well, look at the way you're shaking right now," Katrina says. "And by your own description how things have gone since you started opening up the box and doing medicine. Do you think seven-year-old you could have handled dealing with all that? It is an unfortunate truth that children are most vulnerable to trauma but also least able to handle and process it. All most of them can do in those situations is push down all those bad feelings. And then they fester inside until some part of them is ready to start dealing with it or can't keep all the trapped emotion at bay anymore, like with your pelvis."

She adds that she asked my pelvis what happened and not me because the brain can be tricky, but the body always knows.

"Do you know how it ended?" Katrina asks on the walk.

"He quit," I say. "He loved working with me but had a prior commitment."

"Hmmm," Katrina says quietly. "Your higher self will meter out what it thinks you can handle."

I begin referring to Mr. Bishop as my rapist. Katrina says referring to him that way gives him a lot of power, and we should give him a nickname that signifies how weak he truly is. We settle on "Dickhead" over my original choice of "the Motherfucker."

Katrina is concerned about me being alone right now, but I am adamant I am going home.

That night, she sends me a list of things to help me over this next period:

- Journaling
- Taking hot baths
- Going on walks in nature
- Calling friends
- Talking to Bruce
- Talking with my mom
- Taking supplements
- Eating good, nourishing food

When I get home, I'm not sure what to do. I am disturbed by how unfazed I am about everything. It still feels like a bad dream I will soon wake from.

Eventually, I fall asleep and have a horrible dream about Dickhead. When I wake up, I immediately go to the toilet and start dry heaving, trying to get the horrible taste of his semen out of my mouth.

Katrina sends several texts checking in and reminds me to call my mom. I have never been less excited to make a phone call in my life.

When I call, she is pulling out of the Trader Joe's parking lot. I get straight to the point. "Mom," I say in a soft voice. "Mr. Bishop sexually abused me when he was giving me piano lessons. I need you to come to Austin as soon as you can."

There is a long pause.

"Okay. I'll be right there," she eventually says. There's an implicit agreement between us to talk more when she gets there instead of on the phone.

I don't know anyone else in Austin. It is still not registering very well. I send my friends a rambling text late that night saying that I was sexually abused.

My mom arrives the next morning. We decide to go for a walk around Lady Bird Lake. It takes me a second to warm up, but I eventually tell her Mr. Bishop has raped me multiple times, and he choked me—and that is why I have been having pelvic floor problems for so long.

She is shocked, even with yesterday's lead-in. She asks me a couple of questions about details but is not dismissive. She thought about it on the airplane and recalls him driving me home for a while and that she and my dad left me alone with him at our house at times. I never feel like she doesn't believe me, just that she does not know what to say.

For the first time, I start to cry a little bit on the walk. I tell her, "I am proud of who I am, and I am going to be okay."

It feels like what I am supposed to say to reassure her and myself, even though deep down I am not sure I believe it.

When we get back from the walk, we are both reeling. My mom starts cooking, announces she will be staying for a while, and sets up on my couch.

# The Beginning

D ickhead and I sat at the piano one early evening in the winter of my first-grade year. It was pitch black outside, the tiny lamp the only light on. His hand was resting on my knee. No one else was home.

He told me he wanted to try something on the floor.

I followed his lead and was on all fours looking out the window into my darkened neighborhood when he raped me for the first time.

He took me to the bathroom, cleaned me up, and told me that this would be our secret. We went right back to practicing the piano like nothing had happened.

I did not say anything to anyone. I lacked the ability to understand, let alone articulate, what had occurred.

We kept doing lessons every Wednesday. Dickhead complimented me at every turn, always affirming my thoughts and feelings, telling me how smart I was and how great I was doing.

My mom went back to work and was rarely around. My dad was usually home in other parts of the house, except when he was driving my baby brother to my mom so she could stay at the office longer.

Later that year, Dickhead told my mom that he was often waiting for me at our house because the bus took so long and that he was always getting stuck on the interstate driving back into the city after our lessons. He wondered if he could drive me home from school on lesson days. That way, we could leave right when school was over, and we could start right when we got to my house. There was less wasted time for both of us, and he could get a jump on the traffic going home.

It was billed as a convenience, a favor to him.

My mom signed off. I was excited; I hated the bus and liked Dickhead. I had already established him in my mind as a friendly person, an authority figure, and someone who had provided months' worth of evidence that he liked me. The isolated incident that I did not understand was already banished to the far corners of my mind.

I started going to find him every Wednesday, walking with him to his car in the school parking lot as kids left for the day in every direction.

In the car, he had total control in a way he did not at my house. He decided where we went, when we arrived at my house, and the emotional state I was in when we arrived.

The first time he drove me home, he took me for a gas station candy bar. I felt special.

But the next time, we drove to a park five minutes from my house (today, the park's website refers to it as "pristine wilderness"). He pulled the car into the darkened woods, past the parking lot, not a soul around on a Wednesday afternoon.

It all happened so fast. He was in and out of the backseat in what felt like seconds.

Before I knew it, we were pulling up to my house for our lesson.

He never acknowledged that anything was out of the ordinary. He was cheerful the entire time.

Once, while it was happening, I asked what he was doing, and he said he didn't know what I meant. I didn't trust myself to say anything further.

I kept looking for how whatever was happening could be a positive. Maybe this was something he did to show he liked me?

This continued for a number of rides. But as we drove out of the woods one Wednesday toward the end of the school year, I told him from the backseat that I didn't think I liked what just happened and wanted it to stop.

There was a pause.

And then he turned around from the front seat, his face darkened, his eyes narrowed. His voice changed.

He told me this was happening because I was a bad kid and that if I told anyone, everyone else would find out what a bad kid I was, and my mom would hate me.

He said no one loved me, not even my mom, which was why she did not spend any time with me, and that my dad had no idea what to do with me. That I was not like everyone else and that was why all the other kids in our music class hated me.

He even mentioned the globe I brought to school and once proudly showed him as evidence that I was not like them, that I was a freak.

I was stunned.

He said it all so quickly. What he said didn't make any sense. I had to be mishearing.

But then his voice changed back. He went on for minutes about how smart and amazing I was. I was reassured. I *had* misheard him before. Now things made sense again.

We arrived at my house and did the lesson as we always did.

It kept going like this.

He was as kind and as friendly as could be as we got into his car every Wednesday. Except now, we always stopped at the woods before we went to my house, where his dark side briefly emerged before changing back.

Early on, he drew enough blood that he took me to a gas station bathroom to clean me up. When this happened again, we went to the same gas station, and he switched out my underwear.

He seemed to watch my reactions. Over time, he homed in on my mom, continuing to tell me that she would hate me if anyone found out and that he would kill her if I told anyone.

He repeated a variation of these manipulations over and over again every week, the auditory repetition sinking into my developing brain, before his friendly side came back as we started leaving the woods toward my house.

There were what felt like elements of truth to everything he said. I did feel like there was something different about me. I did feel like an outcast. And I did have doubts about both of my parents.

Dickhead brought those doubts, my underlying fears, to the surface.

The way he effortlessly switched in seconds between mean and nice, between threatening to kill my mom and telling me I was his favorite kid in class, frightened and bewildered me. I didn't know what to believe.

*Was he really saying that? Why would someone who was so nice to me say that? Why would an adult, a teacher, say that to me? Why would someone my mom liked, who she said liked me, and who she sent me home with say that? Did he know something I didn't? Did he know I was a bad kid?*

I still did not trust myself. What was happening did not make sense to me, so I decided I was wrong.

Occasionally my mom was home when Dickhead and I got there, happy to see us. Seeing how nice she and Dickhead were to each other made me feel like what he was doing to me was okay. It also hurt that she did not notice my bewilderment coming home from those rides.

Over time, it was so scary and disorienting that I started blacking out during the rides home. I put what happened on those drives home in a box. I could still pretend it wasn't happening.

I had so much readily available evidence that he liked me. The way he laughed with me every piano lesson, music class, most of the drive home. But over time, the abuse began to sink in, even if I did not know why.

I started crying even more at school, which led to more bullying. Toward the end of the year, my dad got mad about how often I came home from school upset. He angrily called my teacher, yelling at her that he did not understand why I was coming home sobbing every day. They agreed I was sensitive and was being bullied. She vowed to be nicer to me moving forward.

Around that same time, I saw the school counselor. I did not mention Dickhead, but I told him I hated school. I didn't want to be here, and everyone here hated me. The counselor was a kind man. He never made me feel like any of this was my fault or that he was mad at me in any way. He told me that I was bright and mature and over time the other boys would catch up to me.

But I did not feel heard. After a couple of meetings, he talked to my parents. They got along well. He told them he thought I was going to be fine and that I was just having some initial trouble adjusting.

I saw him once or twice at the very beginning of second grade, and we ran into the exact same problems, both of us repeating similar patterns. Even as a seven-year-old I could tell he was not hearing me the way I wanted to be heard.

Everyone around me—from him to my teacher to my parents —started with an assumption that I was sensitive, being bullied, and struggling to adjust. And every question, every concern felt like a way for them to reaffirm their preconceived notions about what the problem was.

Honestly, I am not sure I was capable of articulating what was happening, even if someone had asked.

When I look back at first grade, it felt like I got hit by a tidal wave. The damage that year was as much psychological as physical. In the car Dickhead had plenty of time to deny my reality, to get me to doubt myself, what I was seeing and feeling at every turn, all while chipping away at my self-esteem. I began to believe there was something wrong with me that he was seeing inside of me. I lost confidence in myself, especially with anything related to him.

I was uncertain about what was really going on the entire year, looking for any and every reason to doubt myself and believe his nice side.

But by the end of the year, I was terrified of him.

And then it got worse.

# Sinking In

In the period following the uncovering of the rapes, I struggle to think about anything else. I think about it in the morning when I wake up. I think about it when I'm working. I think about it before I go to bed every night.

My mom stays for a while, and then friends and other family visit. I am able to laugh and joke with them at times. I am also grateful to be working as a distraction. But even when my mind leaves the abuse for a second, it always comes jumping right back, often without me even realizing it.

*How did I not see this?* I ask myself. In hindsight, it all seems so obvious. The guardedness, the fear around touch, and most of all, my years of horrible pelvic problems.

My background threw me off. My parents have never come anywhere close to physically abusing me. Even in my extended family, no one has ever been accused of any sort of crime or is weird like that. I did not grow up in any sort of perceived danger.

But I also felt a sense of arrogance that I would never let myself get raped. And that if I had been raped, I believed of course I would have remembered. It is scary and disorienting to realize I had not.

None of my practitioners seem surprised. In fact, it feels like they all saw it long before I did. But I am frustrated with some others around me—I feel believed by everyone, but I also sense a skepticism, that I had known my whole life I had been raped and just picked now to start dealing with it.

Until the days after the disastrous MDMA session with Amy, I didn't have the slightest idea I ever could have been sexually abused. Even in the period between that session and when I started working on it, I denied I had ever been raped, even to myself. But then I look at how many trauma books I read and how often I googled Dickhead's name and see that once I started consciously denying it, a deeper part of me began preparing for the truth.

Before that, it just didn't compute. If I'd known I was raped, I never would have stuck a wooden stick up my ass.

If I had known I had been raped, especially once I became aware of psychedelics, the first question I would have asked myself is, *Why wasn't I using these compounds to try to heal?*

Some part of me was not ready to take that drastic step right up until the moment I was.

I am exhausted and on edge all the time, especially on days when I do therapeutic work around the abuse. Things happening in the world that I used to care about suddenly seem so trivial. Sometimes all I can do is lie down on my couch, aimlessly scrolling through social media or dating apps.

Strangers feel threatening in a way they didn't before. Even just walking around my neighborhood, my first reaction when I pass someone is to think through all the ways they could hurt me, carefully watching them out of the corner of my eye.

The memories of the abuse are like water out of a faucet. Before the session, they had come back in the tiniest of trickles. Now, after, it feels like the faucet has been turned on full blast, stronger than I want or need.

I dread going to sleep. Seemingly every night, I have some sort of bad dream. Dickhead choking me. Dickhead threatening to kill me. Dickhead telling me no one would believe me. A reoccurring one is that I had gotten a sexually transmitted disease from the rapes and would slowly die from it, the doctors telling me there was nothing they could do for me, just like they did with my pelvis.

When I wake up in the middle of the night after dreaming about him and hearing his voice, usually in a panic, things he said or did come back to me in a flood.

And it's not just Dickhead. I dream of driving my car off the road before waking up terrified. In multiple instances I wake up convinced there is an intruder in my apartment, and I frantically get up, turning everything over, and making sure the door is locked, still half asleep. Another time, my mom wakes me up because she heard me yelling from the other room. Once I wake up with my pelvis burning, except this time I know exactly what I was dreaming about.

There's not much to do when I have these kinds of dreams except try to calm down and go back to sleep. When I feel really bad, I go for a walk around my block in the middle of the night.

I journal regularly to try to make sense of it.

I continue to see Katrina each week. During an energy session, it comes up in a visceral way for the first time. I go into such a tail-spin I can't drive home and have to rely on my one friend who has just moved to town to pick me up and stay with me for the night.

In the weeks after the session, I struggle with anger—the kind of deep, shaking anger where my fists and jaw clench and my back tightens. I fantasize about shattering Dickhead into a million pieces or choking him and watching his eyes go wide the same way I know mine did when I was small.

I've never felt anger consciously like that before. But with that anger comes not empathy but more of an understanding of how sexual abuse victims can turn into abusers—it's rare, but it happens, and now I begin to see why. My anger is always directed at him, and to some extent my parents, never on innocent children. But I am mad enough that I can see how if someone was not loved and then was victimized this way, they could have enough rage and be in such pain to become a perpetrator.

When I look at my body, I hate everything about it—scrutinizing every pore, obsessing over the slightest imperfections, like the tiny scars on my hips that in my mind take up my whole leg. I feel gross and disgusting, that the most intimate spaces of my body have been violated—because they have.

There are moments of self-pity. *Why me?* I wonder. *What did I do to deserve this?*

I constantly relitigate my life. By the time I met most of my friends, by the time my sister was born, by the time I was John Smith in the third-grade play, I'd already been raped.

*What if my parents had bought a house in a different school district? What if they'd just stayed separated? What if I'd never signed up for piano lessons?*

Katrina tells me that these thoughts, this why-me self-pity, are an important part of the healing process, that they come from the wounded child part of me that had been victimized.

But she also says that it's important not to get stuck in pity, that it's a phase to go through and come out of, not a permanent part of my identity.

The blame starts coming in as well. *How could my parents have let this happen to me? How could I have let this happen to me?*

I struggle to cry about the rapes.

What sustains me is loathing Dickhead. The situation gives me a clear enemy in a way I have never had one before. I feel like he bested me, the same way I felt when I lost in sports. I am determined not to let that motherfucker ruin my life.

I plow that sense of purpose into healing.

I'm quickly ready to do MDMA again. I still have concerns about what actually happened and how bad it was.

My nervous system still feels fried, and my dick still does not work. Deep down, I know I have a long way to go.

Katrina, my mom, and I decide that my mom will fly in and come pick me up after sessions in the future. I meet with Katrina and Chester in the healing room, where Katrina says, "Whatever happens today, we will go at the pace your psyche wants to go."

And then we are off.

The last session I was not able to get very far beyond certainty that he had raped me. This time, however, I am peering down from above, like I have a bird's-eye view. I see myself at the piano with Dickhead and feel the shock to my system when he raped me for the first time. And then the bird's-eye view suddenly disappears.

The next several hours, it comes back in images and incomplete details rather than full memories or stories. But nothing is left to the imagination this time. There are no complaints that I can't see anything; it is all there, albeit in disorganized form. In the back of his car. At my house. In his classroom. The worst thing that ever happened to me starts coming back for the first time on medicine this session.

There are moments I can feel my own shock about what is coming out of my mouth. Sometimes, I can hear Katrina waver a bit in surprise. I do briefly dissociate a couple of times, in much the same way I would doze off for a nap for a second before jolting back awake. But I trudge through it, sometimes describing it as casually as I would describe the weather, the only hints of its heaviness the occasional shock and trembling in my voice and my whole body shaking.

The peak of an MDMA session is about ninety minutes long, before gradually dimming from there. At the peak, anything that comes up feels mostly okay in that moment, the safety of the medicine overpowering any negative emotions.

But as the MDMA starts to wear off, thoughts of Dickhead begin to fade, and I start to grasp how devastated I am about what I have spent the last several hours laying out. I throw a temper tantrum, slamming my fists over and over on the bed.

"Why isn't this fucking working!" I yell, still very much in shock. "It just keeps getting worse."

"It's starting to sink in now, isn't it?" Katrina asks.

"Yes, it is," I reply numbly.

"This is going to take a while," Katrina says. "I know there are people who say one session changed everything for them, but I don't think that is a realistic expectation given what you went through and how young you were when you went through it."

"I promise it is working," she adds. "Your whole body shook like a leaf today. That is your nervous system releasing some of the trauma and resetting itself. But we are still at the very beginning, so I understand why you can't see it."

I realize one of the reasons I am getting so frustrated. "MDMA isn't going to be enough for me, is it?" I ask.

"Probably not, no," Katrina says. "You've gotten a lot of mileage out of it. You needed to start there, but it is too friendly to get where you ultimately need to go. MDMA is best at pulling up trauma—trauma that your brain has spent your whole life pretending didn't happen and refusing to look at—in a gentle way, resetting the nervous system, feeling self-love sometimes for the first time. But those are just the first steps. And it can't always get into the deeper layers of your psyche because everything comes in so gently."

I mention a therapist I have been working with who keeps talking about ayahuasca, but I am not getting the sense that would be good for me. (We did not end up working together long.)

"Aya was transformative for me later on, but aya is a big gun. For where you are now, aya will fuck you up," Katrina says matter-of-factly. "The ego is like a rubber band—yours is very tight, and it is good to be stretched, but stretch it too far, too fast, and it could snap."

"Do you think I should try psilocybin?"

"It will always be your choice, but that is where I would go next if I were you," Katrina says. "Mushrooms can be really good at getting beyond the intellectual and at the deeper emotions and the unconscious programming these events left you with. 'I don't matter' or 'I am shameful' are thought patterns. Stories that were drilled into you and stories you told yourself to make sense of why this was happening. They are not true, but because they were so ingrained in the early years, they became part of your default settings as an adult.

"Mushrooms can reset your mind and give you the opportunity to experience new ways of seeing yourself, with a different internal framework—a software update, so to speak. 'I am shameful' turns into 'That is not my shame.' 'I am broken' turns into 'I have scars, but I am healing.' 'I am not good enough' turns into 'I am doing my best, and I have love and compassion for myself.' Until one day you will look at these old patterns and see through them for what they are: thoughts that are no longer serving you."

We keep chatting as I ease my way out of how rough today was, like a cool-down after an intense workout, until I take the mask off to get some food.

I haven't eaten anything since last night, and I stuff some fruit in my mouth. As Katrina goes to grab Chester's leash for our walk, I start to feel dizzy enough that I have to lie back down. As I am lying there, I realize everything is going to come back up right now. I scramble to the bathroom and don't quite make it to the toilet. I have vicious, whole-body heaves, worse than any food poisoning I have ever had. The only thing saving me is there is not much food in my stomach.

I am lying in the fetal position in my underwear, in Katrina's bathroom, exhausted and demoralized, head now resting on my shoulder as she works around me, cleaning up the mess. I never make it out for the walk.

My mom pulls up. My clothes are covered in throw-up, so I have to wear some of Katrina's. It is the first time my mom has ever seen me right after an MDMA session. She looks surprised. When I get in the front seat, she tentatively asks how it went in a way that suggests she already knows the answer.

"It was a rough fucking day," I say and lean my head against the passenger window. As we drive away, my mom starts crying a little bit before stopping herself. We otherwise spend the entire drive back to my apartment in silence, stuck in rush-hour traffic.

I realize that I'd held onto the expectation that I could move through what happened in months, maybe a year, and that it wouldn't impact my life long term. Today's brutal session broke those expectations for good. Maybe the rapes won't prove to be life *defining*, but they will forever be life altering. And I'm beginning to understand that true healing is not going to take months or a year but a long time.

When I get home, I go to my room and lie down, my body exhausted, mind whirling, listening to my mom doing laundry in the background. I wish that this could all be a bad dream I will one day wake up from—but for the first time I accept that I never will.

# Second Grade

There were almost thirty of us again in my second-grade class, but I was still a loner. My teacher was pushing sixty and struggled to remember my name. She also seemed to come from an era when children were more seen than heard. Her attitude was that teachers were adults and adults always knew best.

At 3:30, the last class of the day finished, and the pack-up to go home began. At 3:45, the bell rang, ending the school day. At 4:00, the buses were called over the loudspeaker. It was a chaotic time in school, especially in my classroom.

Early in the year, Dickhead arrived at my classroom door as the last class of the day was ending. I discovered he had already arranged with my teacher to come get me for "afterschool piano lessons" in his classroom. We were still doing piano lessons every week at my house.

He'd never tried this the previous year.

The first time he arrived, my teacher told me to go with him, and I was scared enough of him that I did. No one had any reason to suspect him of anything.

His music room was large, windowless, away from all the other classrooms, near the front entrance of the building. We started at the piano, practicing just like at home. After what felt like only a minute or two, he told me that he wanted to try something on the floor. By now, I knew exactly what that meant.

At the end, as the buses started to be called over the loudspeaker, he started in on the threats toward me and my mom. He never named what was going on, but he told me that no one would believe a boy like me. He also said that if anyone ever asked where I was and I did not say piano lessons, he would kill me.

The friendly side of him returned as I was leaving. His compliments centered around my intelligence and physical appearance. My green eyes, my smile, and my auburn hair. He told me I was a great student and we would do lessons again tomorrow. I left straight from his classroom to go home on the bus.

He kept coming back to my classroom right as the school day was ending. We just had to make eye contact—he had already done so much damage, instilled so much fear going back to the car the year before—that when he did arrive at my classroom, I never protested and went with him quietly.

Over time, when we went to pack up for the day, I did not come back to class and started hiding in the bathroom or wandering around the building, trying not to run into him or draw attention to myself. I was already scared and ashamed. I felt like it was my fault this was happening. I just had to make it until the buses were called.

Dickhead had a class until 3:30, but afterward he would come out, power walking around the school, looking for me.

The second I saw him, I submitted. He would put his hand on my shoulder like he was supporting me, but I found it menacing. Plenty of people saw us. I don't remember anyone ever discussing this sort of behavior beyond telling groups of us never to get in the car with strangers.

I wanted it to stop, but I just as desperately didn't want anyone to find out.

Sometimes it took a while for him to find me. We would speed walk to his room right as the bell rang for the day, hustling to the piano for what felt like thirty seconds and then right to the floor.

And on Wednesdays it was my job to find him so he could drive me to our real piano lesson at my house.

That year, he started mixing in threats right when we got in the car. He would tell me how smart I was or how much my parents must love me. Seconds later, he'd say that I was stupid and that everyone hated me before raping me in the woods. There would be times when we would arrive at my empty house, which gave him more opportunities to abuse me—and also made me feel like what he was saying was true.

There were some days in the first month of second grade that I managed not to run into him, but it never stopped or ended. As things got worse, I became more and more ashamed. I was seven years old and still not sure what was happening—just that it was scary and all my fault, and I could not tell anyone.

When I look at my second-grade year, it was less about manipulation and more about submission.

One Wednesday, I took the bus home instead of finding him to drive me. He was already parked in my driveway as I walked up. He did not acknowledge anything was amiss. My dad was home, and Dickhead and I walked into my house together. Dickhead was all smiles.

The next day, things started to turn. When the last class ended, he was already outside, bolted to the spot, staring at me.

I went with him and got raped as usual, but things were different afterward. I had never seen him so mad. He told me that if I ever did not find him when I was supposed to, he would kill me.

And then he choked me for what felt like a couple of seconds, his eyes full of anger as he did so.

Then, just as quickly, he let go. His eyes settled. His friendly voice came back, and he said he would see me tomorrow to continue our lessons.

After that, there was no more resistance. I stopped thinking and just complied. When we went to our cubbies to pack up, I slipped out and headed straight to his classroom. It was just like going to another class. I found him every day except on days when I walked into his classroom and he was already occupied.

All the rapes from this period run together, the way morning bus rides or brushing my teeth run together. There was a part of me that left my body before I even got in the room. It was all so quick and routine. We started at the piano, and by then I went to the floor before he even had to say anything. Afterward, he cleaned me off. My bus was called, and I went home from there. Like clockwork.

It did not hurt that much. Sometimes I looked back, and he wasn't really doing anything. His eyes were closed like he was asleep. It felt like I was not even there.

But when I was performing oral sex on him, he often forced me to make eye contact with him.

Over time, he started to ejaculate on my face. He drew blood regularly and wiped it off my butt or wiped semen from my face with tissues that he kept. As we finished, he usually choked me.

I found the more he choked me, the more compliant I was, until the point where he did not have to do it anymore.

Most of the time I don't think anyone noticed I was gone. I had no friends, and my teacher was long in the tooth. But I know that at least once, if not more times, she asked where I was going, and I reminded her that I had piano lessons after school. Part of me genuinely believed I was going to piano lessons because the alternative was too scary. But I also went up to her desk and expressed to her at various points that I did not like going to piano lessons. She told me that was between me and Dickhead, not something she would be getting involved in.

The worse it got, the less I wanted to tell anyone. It was like a lie that got bigger and bigger, a hole that got deeper and deeper. An ever-increasing cycle of fear and shame.

Unlike first grade, I did not cry much that year. By then I was too shut down. I never collapsed or refused to go to school. When I got home from school, I immediately retreated to my room or the basement. I watched movies every day that year. I was terrified and ashamed that anyone, but especially my parents, would find out. So I started trying to subtly disappear in my own home.

My mom found out early in the year that she was unexpectedly pregnant again. The internet bubble had crashed, and the company she was president of was tanking. She worked nonstop that year and traveled often. Even when she was home, she was preoccupied and taking care of my brother.

I also wanted to put my best foot forward for her in particular because I didn't want to have her hate me or put her in danger, both of which Dickhead reinforced and I believed would happen if she found out.

I suspect if pushed, my mom would have said of course my brother and I were her first priorities. But her actions throughout my early childhood and especially that year suggested otherwise.

My dad was home most of the time, but he did not seem to read my verbal cues or expressions very well. Sometimes I feel like he almost could not see me. I would not say being a nonjudgmental listener was one of his strengths.

At one point, my parents did try to have an intervention. They were concerned with how much time I was spending alone and how I was doing. I could feel their judgment, as I could with most adults during this period. I told them that I liked being alone and was doing okay. I was determined to put on a better face for them. They debated sending me to a different school or taking some sort of action but did not.

There were plenty of moments when I truly had no idea what was going on. It was so scary, and I was so terrified of him that my brain couldn't process what was happening.

But there were other times I could see it more clearly.

Like when I told a reoccurring babysitter that I did not like doing piano lessons with him, and while she was sympathetic, she replied that most boys do not like piano in a way that made me feel like she did not hear me.

Or when I had a full-on meltdown at a soccer teammate's birthday party, my parents not there, and no one knew what to do. Waking up in the middle of the night terrified. Crying on the playground. Sitting by myself on the bus.

I could have said something that year, but due to a mixture of shame, fear, and not wanting to hurt anyone else, I choose not to say anything directly to anyone during this period. (While my parents were not paying attention to me or my emotions, I am certain that had I told either one of them that Dickhead was touching me inappropriately, they would have taken immediate action.)

I turned eight years old in November, very much entrenched in this horrible pattern.

# Doubling Down

The day after I throw up at my MDMA session, I am visiting with friends from out of town. They are chatting about their jobs, girls, things I normally would have contributed to. But today I am not there, my mind still rolling.

*How can I possibly explain to anyone what happened yesterday?* I think. *What this has all been like for me?* They know I had been raped and at one point offer to talk about it, but I pass both because I do not think they're ready to hear the grim details and also because I don't want to discuss it.

Since recognizing the abuse, I feel like I'm on an island, like there is an invisible barrier between me and much of the world. It's not anything anyone says or does; I just find the rapes hard to discuss with most, despite it being all I can think about.

Katrina is firm in my integration session the following week. "It is fucked what happened here. You were victimized. It is unfair. But I think part of becoming an adult is learning that life is unfair and all anyone can do is the best with what has been put in front of them. So we can commiserate all day about how fucked it is, but I don't think that will help you heal."

I'm nervous as I head back home to northern Virginia for Thanksgiving. Thankfully, a few years before, we moved out of the house I was raped in, but my family still lives in the same county.

I haven't told many people or provided much detail, but I know I'm going to see friends in person for the first time since telling them and that I'll break the news to others.

All my practitioners have cautioned me that people respond in all sorts of ways to sexual abuse and to try not to take anyone's response personally. They warned that some might doubt me or try to minimize the situation, either due to a lack of empathy or discomfort or in some cases to avoid thinking about their own suppressed abuse.

I'm not sure what I want to hear from my friends or extended family on this topic. I guess some acknowledgment of what I had been through would be nice, but most of all, I do not want pity. I hate projecting weakness, and everything about this situation makes me feel weak. I'm also concerned about people not wanting to be around me because of how much I'm struggling with the situation.

Almost all my family and friends are supportive, even if they rarely bring it up or don't quite seem to know what to say. My sister, who I am not super close with, tells me that she is there to talk and support me no matter what.

But I am frustrated by my dad's response. Despite my mom informing him of the basics shortly after I told her that Mr. Bishop had raped me, he and I have barely spoken in the two months since then, and never about that. He does not address the situation at all the first few days I'm home over Thanksgiving.

When we do eventually go for a walk, he begins by complaining that I have not been nice to him since I returned home for the break. In terms of my abuse, he seems to be in denial, clearly uncomfortable, and mostly shying away from discussing the situation.

But at one point he starts crying and says that he felt like a horrible father in a way that, to me, seems less like an apology and more wallowing in his own self-pity, like he's the one who has been victimized here. Perhaps it's my own programming, but I feel like it's my job to reassure him that he had not, in fact, been a bad father, in much the same way an adult would comfort a child.

The walk is the only time all week we even indirectly discuss the rapes. I never hear any sort of accountability from him while I'm home.

While his behavior surprises me, I'm not shocked by it. I feel that his self-centeredness and lack of awareness offers a window into how he had missed me being serially raped in the first place.

By the end of Thanksgiving week, I'm ready to return to Austin.

In the period that follows, I double down on getting help. At Katrina's urging, I find a group in the Austin area for men who have been sexually abused. While we all have different stories, the issues we face are similar.

I still think the deepest healing is done in a one-on-one environment. But I find my group to be a good complement to the individual work I'm doing. I attend weekly sessions for nine months.

I also start doing eye movement desensitization reprocessing, or EMDR.

EMDR involves using bilateral stimulation to try to work through traumatic memories. I hold buzzers in both hands that alternate vibrating between them while focusing on traumatic memories and the emotions behind them with a therapist. The idea is the vibrating, or bilateral stimulation, helps engage different parts of the brain and process trauma.

It's hard to assess how effective EMDR is for me. But I notice I always feel exhausted the rest of the day, and even the next day after a session, so I feel like something is happening.

After one EMDR session, I completely lose my voice for days, and I can tell it's related to the memory I worked through. In another instance, I have horrible diarrhea that begins an hour after an EMDR session.

I don't think EMDR alone is anywhere near enough for me to heal. I needed psychedelics to bring up the abuse at all. I still think the medicines and the work I do with Katrina around it are most effective for me. But I find EMDR to be a good complement to those modalities.

I also work with Bruce for one-on-one therapy.

I continue to see my body worker, sometimes several times a week, doing a combination of Pilates and myofascial release through massage. Because my body issues are the result of repressed emotions, physical manifestations of being repeatedly violated, doing body work alone would not have been that useful for me.

While my pelvis is definitely the tightest and most disconnected, much of my body was feeling that way. The physical movement is a great way to reintegrate and start getting back in touch with my body, stretching tense muscles, releasing tight tissue, and reminding myself that my body is still capable of many things, even if certain parts are not working correctly. It's also good for me to have someone I trust with my body, where I can relax and not worry about being violated or uncomfortable.

But the deepest work I'm doing is breathing with Katrina on her table for two hours every Tuesday evening. As some of the shock wears off, more anger takes its place. So to start the sessions, I bang on her drum to try to get some of it out.

"Anger is a secondary emotion. It is the top layer," Katrina says. "People who are angry are using their anger to mask something else, usually fear or sadness. When you can get past the anger into primary emotions, that is when you can start to move through things."

But even with the drumming, I frequently find myself pissed off in these sessions.

I'm reliving every time someone has ever screwed me over, going all the way back as far as I can remember. I explain why they did that to me and what was wrong with them. The evenings sometimes turn into full-blown grievance sessions.

Katrina and I had a honeymoon period when we first started doing medicine, but as that wears off and I get angrier, there is often friction between us. Some sessions, we get along great; I'm able to work through things breathing on her table, and we hug goodbye. But there are multiple-week periods where we argue most of the session, and it does not feel like things are going well. I leave her house cussing under my breath, never considering quitting but not excited to come back next week.

In one sense, I feel safe to let it all out with her in a way I do not with anyone else. But she also seems to have a unique way of triggering me.

I never feel like she doesn't care, but I often think she is being unfairly tough and that I'm somehow not doing something right in a way that triggers my perfectionism. I constantly worry I am failing and that I will be stuck angry, alone, and with a limp dick forever.

Katrina had a traumatic childhood, but she was not raped. When I feel defensive, I tell her that I'm skeptical she would be where I am if something like what happened to me had happened to her. She often mentions that developing a spiritual practice was a big way she got herself out of depression, and I dismiss her every time she brings it up, feeling like she is implying I'm somehow falling short by not having one.

One night, she casually observes that we have more friction than she has with any of her other clients. I fire back that it's because she mostly works with women. Sometimes we even argue about whether I'm argumentative. It's frustrating when I cannot seem to bulldoze her into agreeing with me and my narrative.

Even when she tells me I'm doing well, I struggle to hear it. She notes that I have a remarkable talent for finding the negative in anything she says.

"Alex, I am not out to get you. I promise," she says in exasperation one night after I yell at her again. "You don't have to trust me. But I don't think you can heal without giving up some control and trusting something other than yourself."

"Like a teacher?" I snark back.

In the months that follow, I struggle with empathy. If it's not about me, I don't care. The feelings come to a head when I deride the concerns of someone close to me as "bullshit" and complain to Katrina that the person in question is "soft as hell."

Katrina sighs as she says, "Judgment feels good—in this case, that you are tough and we are all weak. And you absolutely are tough. But eventually that judgment will leave you looking down on everyone, feeling alone."

As my lack of empathy becomes more glaring, I begin to see that I already had issues with being self-centered long before the rapes came up. When I think of self-absorption, I picture people who dominate the conversation or brag about themselves. I don't have those problems. But I have always had a tendency to take things personally and an obsession about how I am being perceived by others, which I come to realize is self-absorption, just in a different way.

There are moments of self-reflection when I start to see these things. But then I find myself falling right back into the same patterns I was in before.

Katrina never raises her voice at me like I do with her, but at times she can't hide her frustration. "Alex, I have seen you how sweet you can be in your heart, the way I bet you were when you were little. Loving, gentle, warm—like a teddy bear. That's the side of you I see on medicine and even sometimes in here. It is your mind that is rougher, lacking empathy, super judgmental, defensive, guarded, pushing people away. And that comes from trauma. But that's the side I am seeing a lot of right now."

We have a similar sense of humor, one that is on the darker side. "Dickhead was way more into me than any girl ever was," I remark one night, half laughing, half bitter. "I would have killed to have some girls chase me around the building in high school."

Katrina fights back a grin before turning serious. "I have no idea why he picked you. Maybe it's because you were cute, your parents weren't super engaged, you're the one who responded to his ad, or some combination, but I do think it is important to remember that it wasn't personal. You were objectified. It didn't have anything to do with your character or something defective about you."

"It's pretty hard not to take someone repeatedly forcing their dick into your butt personally," I retort, now kind of annoyed.

"I get that," Katrina says. "But I do think you will drive yourself into a ditch if you decide this happened because of something that's wrong with you."

In other sessions I blast my parents.

"Where do they find these people?" I ask sarcastically one night. And then it just keeps going from there. I start speaking faster and faster, my words often laced with profanity. "I was a sitting duck. They are immune to self-reflection and lacking in self-awareness. The thing about not being in touch with your own emotions is it fucks up your radar for other people. Basic questions—like what are the intentions of the guy offering to drive your seven-year-old home?—get missed."

"Do you think you sound like an adult right now?" Katrina asks quietly.

"No," I say with disgust, "and I don't care."

Katrina just gives me a look, so I keep going.

"I have to do all this shit, go to all this therapy, because both of them implicitly refused to look in the mirror and do much of any of it. I am the one paying the price for their weakness. Physical safety is the most fundamental thing parents provide for their kids, and they couldn't do it."

Katrina replies, "Alex, all I'm hearing from you is blame, blame, and more blame. What happened to you was horrible, and you can always hold it over their heads if you want to. But I promise trying to somehow prove how bad a job they did won't get you anywhere."

She goes on. "Let's say you truly did have the worst parents in the world. Where does that leave you now? How does that help you heal? It is not your fault. None of this is your fault. But I would argue healing is your responsibility if you choose it to be. And I do think over time, there is power in taking responsibility for yourself."

I'm silent at that one, so she keeps going. "Blame is another form of being a victim, just like you were when you were little. The worst part is that how hard you are on them, how hard you are really on everyone, I promise is how you feel about *yourself*. Underneath all that anger is a hurt little kid. That is what we're trying to do here on the table with the breath and even with the psychedelics. Blow that hurt out, move the bad energy out, so it stops rearing its head and harming both you and your relationships."

And after what feels like a lifetime of heavy breathing on her table, I do let go of a bit, very much still believing my parents let me down, but with more sadness and even a few tears.

"In their defense, he is still at a school now," I say with a grimace and a shrug as I'm getting ready to leave for the night.

In the days after that breathwork session, the feelings around my parents do not go away, but the edge has been taken off a little bit, like a tiny piece of hurt that was once there is now gone.

And while I still have plenty of anger toward her, I spend the most time with my mom in the months that follow. She flies to Austin every couple of weeks, sometimes to pick me up from psychedelic sessions, but also to cook, hike, drive me to all my appointments, and otherwise support me, sleeping on my couch, visibly the oldest person in my building.

My mom seems to be looking for ways to "fix" the situation and coming up short. It often feels like she is at a loss for how to handle something as squishy and lacking a clear instruction manual as emotions. She repeats robotic clichés, frequently telling me, "You're going to get through this. It's important to move forward and focus on what's in front of you."

It's jarring and frustrating for her to already be so focused on the future when I still feel too much shock and anger to be sad, let alone feel ready to move past it.

At times, I feel she is denying my emotions, trying to tell me how to feel in how determined she seems to move past it, like it was a bad cold and not a life-altering experience. I think that part of the reason she is so determined for me to move on is because it makes her feel bad. Her response reminds me that emotions are not her strong suit. And I see how, especially when she was younger and preoccupied, she could have missed all this.

But she also takes responsibility, in a way I respect and am not sure I could have done if I was in her position.

"It's not like I didn't know him," she tells me. "I let him into our house and let him drive you. He seemed a little odd but otherwise a perfectly nice guy. That he would touch you never would have occurred to me, especially back then."

At least most of the time, I can see beyond the clichés that she is hurting inside.

"The memories I have of that time period, both of who I was as a person and how available I was for you are not good," she reflects one day. "Obviously, I wasn't around enough, and you didn't feel comfortable telling me. And there were things about our family that made him feel like he could do that to you. I do remember you struggling at that time and everyone reassuring us you were going to be fine and otherwise not being concerned. There was a lack of imagination on my part about what could really be going wrong there. My own parents never put a lot of thought into my crying at seven years old."

My mom never questions or discourages any of the work I'm doing, even if I frequently get the sense she wishes it was all happening a little faster. That she chooses to take so much ownership and is supportive makes it easier for me to let go of my anger toward her. I can see that she is stretching herself beyond her emotional comfort zone in any way possible to help me, sometimes conferring with Katrina (with my permission) over ways to best be there for me.

"Well, you guys are definitely the best set of parents in my survivor group," I say as she drives me back from group therapy one night.

My mom gives a dark laugh and says, "Great."

As we pull into my apartment building for the night, I still feel hurt—but it's good to have her there with me.

# The Worst One

It was a school day near the winter holidays of second grade, not a piano lesson day. My mom was out of town again, trying to save her struggling company.

Dickhead arrived at my classroom door early, before the last class of the day was over. All he had to do was show up at the door, and I got up, excused myself, and went with him. It was the first time he had come to get me in a while; I had long ago started finding him. I walked with him to his classroom, thinking I was going to get raped like usual.

But things were different that day. When we got there, we didn't start at the piano. Instead, he asked if my mom was home. I said no. He asked if she was going to be gone the whole week, and I replied that she was. Then he told me he had talked to her to arrange for us to have a special piano lesson that day, and I needed to go with him to his car now. He put his hands around my neck for a couple of seconds. By then I did whatever he said without question.

He never signed me out of school when he drove me home. I followed him out the door toward the teacher parking lot, just as I did on Wednesdays. No one stopped us.

Dickhead popped the trunk, and I put my backpack inside it. As I was climbing into the backseat, I realized there was another man already in the front passenger seat. I had never seen him before.

It felt like the car was moving before I had gotten all the way inside. The other man turned around for a split second. He looked even younger than Dickhead. He had black hair and dull facial features, and he felt scary to me. Other than that quick look, he did not acknowledge me.

As we pulled out of the school, Dickhead told me that the other man was a friend of his but otherwise offered no explanation for his presence. It was "friendly" Dickhead on the drive, smiling, gassing me up, telling me what a great musician I was, how smart I was, letting me pick the radio station. I barely said a word. The other man—who I will call Fuckhead—was silent.

The radio was on, and there was no communication between Dickhead and Fuckhead. But there was a distinct energy in the car.

I think I knew early on in that ride I had made a mistake. My brain felt like it was moving slower and slower, in a panic, like it was frozen. I didn't move and stayed quiet. When we passed the turnoff to my house and kept going, it became clear.

We arrived in the same woods I had been to many times before, and that was when things started to shift. Dickhead drove into a secluded area past the parking lot where I had been before and where cars shouldn't be. Neither of them got out, but they took out cheap-looking cameras.

The car was still running. We all just sat there in the shadows, the radio still on, except now sounds were coming from Fuckhead in what sounded like a low growl.

I heard Fuckhead's raspy voice for the first time as he told Dickhead, with a lisp, that he just wanted to go. Dickhead's voice was different than I had ever heard before. He said he wasn't sure this was a good spot, but he did not move or turn off the car.

I was still sitting in the backseat in silence. There was nowhere to go. Dickhead moved the car ever so slightly.

Fuckhead was starting to get aggravated. He kept repeating that he wanted to go, that this was bullshit, while banging his feet on the floor, his whole body jerking around.

And then, in an instant I would replay over and over in my mind, Fuckhead sprinted out of the passenger seat like he had been shot out of a cannon, opened the backdoor, and flipped me on my stomach, and it started.

Fuckhead made Dickhead seem like Mother Theresa. At some point, Dickhead yelled he had gotten a picture and now it was his turn. Fuckhead did not acknowledge Dickhead and continued. Dickhead yelled several more times that it was his turn. Fuckhead said he was not done. Finally, after Dickhead shouted at the top of his lungs, Fuckhead gave in for a second.

I was way more concerned about where Fuckhead was than whatever Dickhead was doing to me. Dickhead barely got a shot in before Fuckhead returned. It got much worse when he came back. He did not relinquish me again.

He attacked with an animalistic aggression that felt inhuman. As it continued, the grunts got louder and louder, the breathing heavier and heavier. It felt like I was not the only one having an out-of-body experience.

Fuckhead started complaining that I was not making any sound, the frustration visible in his voice.

He began hitting me in the back with his fist, like a jockey whipping a horse heading into the final turn. The hits got angrier. He smacked me in the back of the head at least once. The last thing I remembered before I passed out was Fuckhead yelling, "Why won't he scream?"

He kept going long after I was able to feel anything. I don't know how long it lasted or where Dickhead was during all this. But at some point, it stopped.

When I regained consciousness and started reorienting, Dickhead had his back to me, barricading Fuckhead from the still-open back door. They were yelling at each other. It felt like they had been going on for a bit, like I was coming in during the middle of an argument.

They were so preoccupied that if I were bigger and had not just been brutally raped, I could have run away. My shoes were off my feet, tossed on the floor. The backseat was dark, but I could tell that it was covered in blood, as were all my clothes.

Dickhead said that they were running late. Fuckhead was panting and shouted that he was not finished.

It was just the three of us, alone in the woods. They were loud, but no one was coming to save me. At one point, Fuckhead yelled that I was a squealer and that they should shut me up. That was when Dickhead started shouting back the loudest, shocked at what he was hearing, asking Fuckhead what the fuck was wrong with him.

At another point, Fuckhead made a run at me. Fuckhead was much shorter than Dickhead, and Dickhead pushed him back.

Dickhead told Fuckhead he could not do this. If he tried, Dickhead would make sure everyone knew it was him and he would spend the rest of his life in prison. Dickhead made it clear that *he* was not going to jail for this.

Things felt like they were moving in slow motion for me, the two of them mostly repeating the same things. Finally, Dickhead said that he was not going to let Fuckhead touch me. That was not going to happen.

Fuckhead said again that this was bullshit but got in the front passenger seat in a huff, slamming the door. Dickhead hustled to the driver's side, and we started pulling out of the woods into the parking lot.

I felt like I was sitting on a wet towel, like I did coming home from the pool, except it was my blood. As we were driving out of the woods, Dickhead peered into the backseat for the first time since getting back into the car. He gasped and then started screaming at Fuckhead.

Before today, Dickhead felt all-powerful to me, always in complete control. I was still messed up, but I could tell this was different —I had never seen him like this before.

He looked back at me again in the rearview mirror and turned his head around a couple of times, while still driving the car. He shook his head and started pounding on the steering wheel, still shouting at Fuckhead.

Fuckhead said nothing. He seemed mad he did not get to keep going. Eventually, he began quietly brushing Dickhead off.

The car felt chaotic with all of Dickhead's yelling. I could hear and see what was going on around me but was dazed and too emotionally numb to process it.

While Dickhead was still panicking, Fuckhead turned around and looked at me in the backseat for the first time since getting back in the car. He asked me what the fuck I was looking at, trying to make eye contact with me. I was too dazed and looked right past him. Fuckhead did not like that I was not showing any visible reaction to him.

In another instance that is seared into my memory, Fuckhead tried reaching for me in the backseat, his outstretched arms inches from my face as I drew away in what felt like slow motion, as if I was watching what was happening from somewhere outside of my body.

Fuckhead tried to climb into the back, but Dickhead held him in the front seat with his right hand as we drove through the backroads of northern Virginia.

Eventually, Fuckhead yelled that this was bullshit, slammed on the window with his hand, folded his arms, leaned his head against the passenger window, and began to sulk.

As Fuckhead pouted, Dickhead shouted that this was ridiculous and he could not believe he had brought Fuckhead here.

Dickhead could not stop looking at and talking about the blood. He said that they did not have to worry about me talking, that I knew what would happen if I said anything. But he screamed again in Fuckhead's direction about the blood, asking him how he was going to get the blood off me and out of the car. There was no answer from Fuckhead; he continued to rest his head against the window.

Dickhead switched gears, saying that we were going to clean me up and take me home. He kept repeating it in a way that seemed like he was talking to himself more than either one of us.

We arrived at the gas station that I had been to several times before.

Dickhead parked, turned to me in the back, and told me that if I said anything to anyone, he would kill me. He got out and grabbed his black jacket and a bag out of the trunk. He came to the back door and draped the black jacket over me. It was big, engulfing my whole body, and made me look like I was wearing a dress.

Fuckhead stayed in the car as Dickhead walked me inside, hand on my shoulder like he was my caretaker. Blood dripped down my leg under the jacket.

He got the bathroom key from the clerk. The clerk didn't seem to notice my blank face.

I had not said a word this entire time and did not start now. Dickhead walked me into the bathroom and began cleaning me up, visibly repulsed, dumping gobs of paper towels into the trash and the toilet.

My clothes were ruined, and Dickhead stuffed them and the jacket in the bag. As he finished cleaning me, we made eye contact for the first time since we had left school what felt like a lifetime ago.

Dickhead said if my dad asked, that the clothes were ruined in an art project, repeating the story several times.

Dickhead told me that nobody liked a boy who bled and everyone would hate me if they found out about this. And that my mom would hate me the most.

I nodded and did not say anything else. He walked me out in new ill-fitting clothes, hand still on my shoulder to keep me from running away, even though there was no way I could have.

Dickhead wiped the backseat down before I sat on the side of it that was less covered in blood.

I was much more alert now, my adrenaline pumping, paying attention to the front seat and listening to what they were saying. I could not feel my body at all.

Dickhead started fuming the second we get back in the car and headed toward my house. The radio was off, and the energy was low. Other than Dickhead's voice, you could have heard a pin drop. I could easily see his right hand gesturing in the air from the back. He said that everyone thought they could do what he did, but he was the one actually finding people and doing all the work.

He proceeded to reel off what sounded like a list of names he had "gotten," most of whom I did not recognize, using his hands to count them in much the same way I could recite the presidents I had memorized.

He told Fuckhead that Fuckhead could never get that many people or find someone like me. Dickhead's voice began to rise. Dickhead told Fuckhead that he could not find anyone and that Fuckhead would not be here today without him.

Fuckhead was not even pretending to listen, his head still resting against the passenger window. This only seemed to make Dickhead angrier.

Dickhead's voice sounded different than I had ever heard before, even when he had threatened me.

He told Fuckhead that he wouldn't last two minutes in a school acting like that and complained that Fuckhead had almost destroyed me. Dickhead said he had a reputation here and that these were *his* people, screaming it several times while pointing his right thumb at himself in emphasis.

Dickhead was ranting now. He asked Fuckhead what the fuck was wrong with him. He asked Fuckhead how he was going to get the blood out of his car. He complained that he was going to have to clean up Fuckhead's mess himself. He asked Fuckhead what they would have done if Dickhead did not have clothes. He yelled that Fuckhead could not even take a picture without going crazy.

There was no response to any of this. Fuckhead looked like he was in the fetal position now, leaning against the passenger window, occasionally making what sounded like a whimper.

Dickhead's anger hung in the air. His right index finger wagged. His whole body emoted. It had the feeling of an angry teacher lecturing the class, all while knowing no one was listening to them.

The tirade toggled back and forth with Dickhead threatening and shaming me in the backseat. He told me that everyone would hate me if anyone found out about this and that the only way I would live is if I did not tell anyone.

We arrived at my bus stop at the top of the hill, Dickhead still midrant, my butt still bleeding. Dickhead opened up the trunk from the driver's seat, looked me in the eye one last time, and told me if I ever said anything about this to anyone, he would kill me.

I got out of the car, grabbed my backpack, and heard them drive away as I started walking the quarter mile down the hill to my house

I never saw Fuckhead again.

# Deciding

Once I dry heave the taste-memory of Dickhead's semen over my toilet, I know I am going to come forward in some way, at some point. As the extent of just how bad the situation was becomes clearer, I am even more determined not to just let this go.

As the winter holidays approach, I begin to move past the initial shock and start thinking about how I am going to do it.

Working with Bruce already feels different after I start working on the rapes. His therapeutic specialty is family systems, not sexual abuse. But things really take a turn once I start talking about potentially going to the police.

Bruce knows the graphic details, and I never feel like he does not believe me. But he has never spoken to the police as part of a criminal investigation—and he is not eager to start.

Several times, he claims to be supportive of me going, but then he spends the next ten minutes, unprompted, going over all the reasons it could be a bad idea for me. He repeatedly brings up a client of his who was raped by clergy members, sued the Catholic Church, and after years of litigation won a settlement. But, in Bruce's telling, the trial was as bad for her as the abuse itself.

I don't think that suing the Catholic Church for money is relevant to me holding Dickhead personally accountable, and I get more and more frustrated every time he brings up this story. At one point,

Bruce speculates that the reason Dickhead had not been caught is because powerful people in the DC area could be protecting him, which I think is ridiculous.

Bruce tells me that he is expressing concern about me coming forward because he cares about me. But he also is providing therapy services across state lines, and it doesn't seem like he wants to get himself tangled up about that with the police. I understand why he doesn't want to be involved and do not hold it against him at all.

I can tell something is being lost in translation by talking over the computer instead of in person because he seems to miss the fact that I have already decided to come forward, with or without him.

Bruce says he believes the best revenge for any victim of childhood sexual abuse is to live well. I'm not going for revenge, but I also do not share his feelings on this.

Most of the time, I think I have the stomach to come forward in a way many survivors understandably do not. I am young, articulate, and stubborn to a fault, with no substance abuse issues, psychiatric diagnoses, or legal problems. I do not need money. And while all childhood abuse is inappropriate, I feel like my situation in particular is worth pursuing further, both because of the severity of what occurred and because I'm certain I was not the only one. Setting aside all the emotional scars, my pelvic floor is still feeling the physical effects of Dickhead's behavior today.

If what happened to me isn't worth coming forward about, what is? And if I'm not the person to do it, who is?

At the same time, my mom interviews people about how to best proceed. Everyone she talks to, including a former FBI agent, tells her the same thing: a crime had been committed, so the clear next step is to go to the police.

My mom decides to call the non-emergency number for the police on a "fact-finding mission" without telling me. After a brief explanation to the person who answers, she is transferred to the Major Crimes Unit. She leaves a detailed message. An officer later calls back. After she asks some purposely vague questions, the officer quickly starts interrogating her. She folds a bit and gives them Dickhead's name. The officer then tells her to have me call him immediately so I can give a statement. My mom refuses to let anyone from the police contact me, but the officer tells her that I need to speak with them as soon as possible for the safety of the community before assigning the case to one of his subordinates.

I have mixed feelings about the police. It is clear to me that they don't always act in citizens' best interests. But I feel that police officers in childhood sexual abuse cases are likely to be in that role because they are passionate about the job and want to do their best to catch child molesters, in much the same way I believe that most surgeons choose that role because they ultimately want to test their skills and operate on people.

So while I anticipate trouble in coming forward with my former and Dickhead's current school district, I believe that, in this particular instance, the Major Crimes Unit and I have similar incentives to do whatever possible to try to bring Dickhead to justice.

But when I hear that my mom has spoken to the police, I get scared.

"I want to come forward at some point," I tell Bruce, "but I'm not sure I'm ready to go *now*."

He nods, like I'm finally saying what he wants to hear. He tells me it's important not to let my mom's guilt drive my decision to come forward, but he says it in such a way that seems to insinuate that is exactly what he thinks is happening.

I have been frustrated with Bruce's thoughts on this issue for a while, but when I get off the Zoom with him that day, I'm seething. It's offensive to my own sense of agency to imply that my mom is driving my desire to get accountability for what happened to me, like I'm some sort of show pony being paraded around to assuage her guilt and not someone nervous but also determined to get justice for myself.

Later in the week, when I am at my angriest, I complain to Katrina that there is no need for Bruce to project his own sense of weakness onto me. I decide that I can no longer work with someone when I do not feel supported on something so important to me.

At the beginning of our next session, I tersely thank Bruce and inform him we will be parting ways. I am mad, but as time goes by, I realize how much of a mess I was right after my first MDMA session and for several months afterward. Bruce was, in many ways, my only support during this difficult time, and for that I will always be grateful.

Katrina neither encourages nor discourages me from going to the police. "There is nothing healed about revenge or vengeance; those reactions always come from a wounded place. To my understanding, if you do decide to go, it's because you are looking for *accountability*. Blame, like what you sometimes do with your parents, is emotional venting and ultimately not productive. Accountability is fact driven and about making sure everyone takes ownership of their own behavior.

"Some people seem to think that the takeaway from psychedelics is that we humans are all one, holding hands and singing kumbaya together. And I believe it is true that all living things, including humans, are part of the same system and come from the same creator. But some people, due to their own pain and unresolved wounding, decide to act out in ways that hurt others. At least to my understanding, society can't function unless adults, in particular, are held accountable for their own choices.

"You know, not so long ago, people would have told you to take a hike if you spoke up about being raped. Now they have to at least pretend to care, even if many lack the empathy to actually do so. In my view, that is a sign of humanity's progress," she says with a dark laugh.

She also tells me, "I would love to go to bat for you, but I just can't. But if going to the police is something you choose to do, then go for it."

# The End of Him

was in shock as I walked home from my bus stop after getting out of Dickhead's car. I don't think he realized the extent to which I was still bleeding. I couldn't feel my body. I didn't know what to do.

My dad and baby brother were home when I got there. I went straight to my room and locked the door. I had my own bathroom, and I decided to run a bath. The water turned red before sinking down the drain.

My dad was downstairs. At one point I thought about calling him up, but I didn't. I was worried about his judgment and thought he would hate me if he found out what a horrible kid I was. And I wanted to keep this to myself.

In the car, I had been able to feel how much Dickhead and Fuckhead hated me. I took that in, internalized it, felt it was my fault. *Something was wrong with me. This happened because of* me. The physical damage made me more ashamed. I thought I would die if anyone found out about this.

I yelled to my dad that I had gotten sick at school and didn't feel like eating dinner. At one point, he tried to come in my room, but my door was still locked. I said I wasn't feeling good and just wanted to sleep, and he told me to let him know if I needed anything. I never saw him face to face that night.

I was so shell-shocked that I don't think I could have said exactly what happened; I just knew that it was my fault and my burden to bear alone.

There was still a lot of blood and bruises on my back. But I didn't feel any pain and thought I was going to be okay.

As the night went on, the adrenaline began to wear off. I had trouble breathing as it got darker. Lying down on my bed in the pitch black, I would think I was okay, like I was coming out of it, but then I would have trouble breathing again and feel dizzy, my heart beating out of my chest. I was going into shock.

It kept going back and forth like this all night. In the worst moments, I could not get up or even move. Several times, I found it so hard to take in a breath that I thought I would black out.

I never went to sleep.

In some ways the aftermath was worse than the event itself.

And while it was my choice to not let anyone in, being alone made things worse.

The next morning, I went right past my dad, barely saying a word, and walked to the bus with a change of clothes in my backpack.

When I got to school, my butt was still bleeding. I still didn't know what to do and eventually asked to go see the school nurse. She was a heavyset woman in her sixties. I told her that something was wrong with my butt and did not elaborate. She looked me up and down once in the front, said my butt looked fine to her, and sent me back to class. I did not try to tell or show anyone else.

The whole week was horrible. My mom was gone. My butt was still bleeding frequently. I brought a change of underwear and shorts to school every day, where I would go to the bathroom stall to clean myself at every opportunity, until my teacher told me I couldn't go anymore. I walked around school panicked all the time that someone would notice the blood seeping through my shorts.

I struggled to sleep and was in a ton of pain. I had trouble pooping and even peeing for a while.

I didn't tell my dad anything and avoided him at every turn, hiding in my room, taking baths every day. But I was totally messed up, that whole week especially, and he didn't notice.

That whole year I was teetering, but I came the closest I ever would to killing myself in the days after.

I still did whatever I could to hide it. It was essential that no one find out. I kept wearing blood-stained underwear to school. I shoved bloody clothes in a plastic bag and threw them away in our garage trash can in the middle of the night, pushing them toward the bottom where they wouldn't be found. I threw away my stained bedsheets, too, waiting to tell my parents I needed new ones until after the trash was gone. At home, I only used the bathroom in my room and cleaned it every day, flushing the bloody toilet paper down the toilet. I was as secretive and meticulous as I could be about destroying evidence and making it look like nothing happened. But I was also hurt that no one noticed.

The part of me doing all the hiding felt disconnected from the rest of me, in much the way I had been going to find Dickhead in his classroom without thinking.

All the times he had raped, choked, and threatened me before made me want to die. But there had never been a moment where I felt my life was actually in danger. Not even close, not even in that stratosphere. What happened with Fuckhead changed everything. The physical damage made it impossible to ignore.

The silver lining was that it broke the bad pattern I was in. I stopped going to find Dickhead at school, and he didn't come looking for me. The next piano lesson, I took the bus home. I had no idea if he would show up, but he did. I let him in, and my legs started shaking the second we sat at the piano. As always when my dad was home, Dickhead praised me the whole time, but I was freaking out. At one point, I started just banging the piano keys, not playing any notes, just making noise, which visibly scared Dickhead.

After that, he completely backed off.

He told my mom he was busy right after school and couldn't drive me home anymore but that I was doing a great job and he loved working with me. My mom never suspected anything.

I started subtly making sure my dad was going to be home for our lessons, knowing I was safe as long as he was there.

Months went by without me getting touched. I didn't have Dickhead for music class that year, so the only time I saw him was for our weekly piano lessons, in which he could not have been kinder. Both my body and my mind started recovering. I thought it was all over.

And then, one day in the spring, without warning, Dickhead showed up at my classroom door as school was ending and made eye contact with me. I followed him to his classroom without question and got raped, but it wasn't the same. I did not black out this time.

I still had never raised a finger against him, never disobeyed beyond avoiding him, and never told anyone directly about what was happening. But after months away, after finally starting to feel like it was over, him coming back terrified me.

He had waited too long. I was out of the unquestioning routine of mindless obedience I had been in before. By then, I was determined to make it stop.

I decided to go to my teacher, standing by her desk at the front of the classroom while my classmates were working on an assignment. I told her that Mr. Bishop was touching me inappropriately during our after-school piano lessons, using the same language my teachers used when we were not keeping our hands to ourselves.

She scoffed and admonished me, telling me that was a horrible thing to say about someone and not something she would tolerate. I went to go sit back down and felt dismissed by her, just like I had with the school nurse.

I had no friends. I wasn't seeing the counselor. No teachers or other adults around me seemed to care, and I had no other support. I was too scared and ashamed to tell my parents.

But I had had enough. It wasn't going to be the same again.

I knew I was in trouble when I walked up to my house and saw that there were no cars in the driveway. It was a piano lesson day in the spring, shortly after I was dismissed by my teacher when I told her that Dickhead had been touching me inappropriately.

No one was home. My house did not have a garage code, and the front door was always locked. But I knew the door on our back deck would be open so I could let myself in. It was the first time in a long time I was home for a lesson by myself.

Dickhead would be arriving soon. I grabbed our home phone and started pacing around the house, unsure what to do. I was already having trouble breathing or thinking straight. I was terrified of something like what had happened with Fuckhead occurring again.

From the piano room window, I watched Dickhead's car pull up the driveway. The phone was still in my hand. I was too scared to dial any numbers and couldn't think of anything else to do.

I walked to the front hall and stood in front of the door, frozen to the spot.

Dickhead knocked. I would not let him in.

He knocked again. My golden retriever Jackson started barking from our enclosed kitchen.

I still did not move. After a couple more knocks, Dickhead peered through the front door window, his hand cupped at his eyebrows, trying to see inside. Our eyes met. He glanced down and saw the phone in my hand.

He started banging on the door now, louder and louder, like he was trying to break it down. Between blows, he would press his face to the window, staring at me. I was trembling so much that the phone fell out of my hand onto the floor.

I couldn't seem to move from that spot, just feet from him, only a locked door separating us.

Suddenly, he stopped knocking. Through the window, I saw him running away from the front door.

I thought he was gone.

Then Jackson, who had been barking the whole time from the kitchen—which was right next to the back door—started barking louder.

And then things happened very fast.

I heard the back door open. I had left it unlocked when I'd come home a couple minutes before. Jackson barked even louder.

Dickhead opened the kitchen door, and his eyes narrowed as they met mine for a split second.

He barreled toward me. At the last second, my feet were *finally* able to move again.

I turned away from him and ran toward the stairs to my room. I didn't make it far.

Because my back was to him, I didn't see his hand rear back. I was not bracing myself when he clocked me in the head from behind with his open hand. It was the only time he ever hit me like that. I immediately fell to the ground.

I was dazed, but even from the floor I could see he was shaking. The phone was several feet away from me. He kicked it farther away and yelled I could never do that.

Dickhead started raping me right there in the front hall, in what felt like a way to try to reassert control and remind me who was boss. I was still out of it.

I was on all fours in the front hall when I started getting it back together. It felt like I had woken up from a long nap. I turned around. The motherfucker had his eyes closed again, in his own world.

I had woken up in more ways than one. I hit him in the face mid-rape, pulled up my pants, and took off for the kitchen door, just feet away. I opened the kitchen door ever so slightly, and Jackson leaped out, running right past me toward Dickhead. I didn't look back, running straight out the back door.

When Dickhead caught up with me on the deck, he was huffing and puffing. He grabbed me, picked me up, and carried me to his car, where he threw me in the backseat before jumping in the front and speeding away.

He tore through my quiet suburban neighborhood. After I had submitted for so long, there was no stopping me now. I tried to climb into the front seat and kept hitting him in any way I could, on the shoulder, the neck, wherever I could reach. He used his right hand to try to push me back into the backseat, his left hand locked on the wheel.

He sped through my subdivision, onto the main road for a minute or two, before pulling over on a darker, quieter side street, not far from my house.

When he stopped the car, I was still trying to hit him. I yelled that something was wrong with him and that I was going to tell my parents. He grabbed my leg and started climbing in the back, yelling at me to shut up. Then he put his hands around my neck.

He strangled me in the back seat of his car on that darkened street. My arms flopped wildly. I could see his panicked eyes staring right into mine as I faded into black.

I don't know what happened while I was unconscious, but I do know that was the last time he ever raped me.

I was eight years old in the spring of 2002 when this horrible chapter of my life ended in the backseat of his car. After he strangled me, all the conscious fear and the horrible association I had of him disappeared to the deepest parts of my psyche, where it stayed for a very long time.

We did one or two more piano lessons when my parents were home, during which he spent the whole time telling me the same empty compliments—how smart and amazing I was and how much my parents must love me. Then he wrote a gushing email to my mom, talking about how much he loved working with me, that I would always be one of his favorite students, and that it was so unfortunate that he now had another commitment after school.

I had Dickhead for music class after this, and he was always exceedingly nice to me. But other than an occasional glance in the hallways, I never spoke to him alone until years later, at my sixth-grade graduation.

My sister was born in May of that year. My brother's birth and hers come close to marking the beginning and end of the rapes.

In third grade, I was still struggling at times, at one point getting bullied badly enough by two girls that my teacher had to say something. Toward the end of the year, long after the abuse was over, each of us wrote and presented a short story in small groups for class. Like everyone else, I presented mine to my group and my teacher, Mr. Wells, who I really liked. Unlike everyone else's story, however, the main character in my story killed himself at the end. At the time, no one said anything, and I thought nothing of it.

That evening, my dad came in and knocked on my door. He said Mr. Wells had called to tell him that I had written a story where the main character had killed himself, and that when a child said something like that, it usually indicated they were unhappy.

My dad said he told Mr. Wells that he thought I just watched too many movies, but he would definitely talk to me about it.

Dickhead wasn't in my conscious thoughts, but I felt like I had been caught doing something wrong. I couldn't agree with my dad fast enough that I had been watching too many movies. I never discussed it again with my dad or anyone else. I was determined that there would never be anything wrong with me.

I spent the rest of my time in elementary school sometimes happy and cheerful but also moody and volatile, even as I started to make some good friends toward the end of my time there.

I left elementary school for good in 2006.

# The Police

A couple of days before Christmas, I fly home to Virginia. I know that while I'm here, I'm going to go to the police.

My mom has already been in communication with the officer assigned to my case. They are in agreement that it's up to me if and when I want to come in. But I'm putting pressure on myself. I still have doubts as to whether now is the right time to go and whether I will be believed. I also have fears about what will happen if they ask me how I remembered all of this. But I feel obligated to go, for no other reason than he is still at a school.

In my medicine session the week before, it became clear that the anxiety about going to the police was distracting me from healing. There was never going to be a "good" time to go, so it was better just to get it over with. After that, I gave my mom the greenlight to schedule me going in.

It's decided I will come in a couple of days after Christmas. I spend the holiday with family, walking laps around my neighborhood alone, not talking about the police but losing sleep over it. I write a couple of formal statements about what I want to say but decide it's better just to go in cold.

The day before I'm scheduled to appear, friends and I head into Washington, DC, to watch football. It's a beautiful, warmer winter afternoon, and we crack jokes at each other's expense and laugh together. For a couple of hours, I mostly forget how nervous I am. This is the best time I've had all year, and I've never been more grateful to have friends than I am in this moment.

It's gray and overcast when I wake up the next morning, which mirrors how I'm feeling.

The police center is an ugly, nondescript government building that are a dime a dozen in northern Virginia. In the waiting room, I'm nervous and jittery, a little too wired on caffeine, my legs shaking from time to time. An officer comes to get me, warmly introduces herself, and makes some light chitchat on the way before planting me in a windowless room where I know I'm being recorded. (There is a link to video excerpts of my statement in the Appendix.)

And then we get started.

I speak about everything I can remember in as much detail as I can. The officer doesn't ask any questions about how I remembered any of this, and while I would have answered truthfully, I see no reason to volunteer that information.

By the end, I feel nauseous from having to go through it all again.

At one point in the interview, the officer tells me, "You need to understand that this is not your fault. Any of it. He is absolutely exactly what you said: a groomer. And I am sorry that it wasn't picked up then."

She later adds, "Alex, I need you to know that you are believed, and I completely understand the dynamics of your trauma."

Before coming in, my mom had told me that the usual next step was to have me call and confront Dickhead on a recorded line with the police listening. But the officer says she will not be asking me to do that.

At the end, she tells me that I'm free to go, and she'll be in touch with my mom about the next steps.

Walking out of the station, everything about life feels darker. After being overcast all day, it starts to rain as we get into the car.

I didn't have a flight back to Texas booked yet because I'd been uncertain about what would happen next. But on the way home from the police station, I panic and tell my mom that I need to get out of northern Virginia as soon as possible. When we get home, I quickly pack my things and head for the airport. On the way, my mom tells me that the police have asked her to call Dickhead, which she may be doing as soon as tomorrow.

Calling him on the phone and trying to get him to confess seems a little strange. But the police do this every day, so I decide they must know what they're doing. My mind keeps jumping around, and I'm very uncertain about this whole situation. I'm also more concerned about getting out of northern Virginia than anything else.

The next few days are strange. I keep replaying my interview in my head. I have a feeling something has happened because my mom is not being very communicative. But I'm halfway across the country—if something major has occurred or if they need me for some reason, I think she or even the police will reach out to me.

Finally, a couple of days later, I break down and call my mom. The first thing she says is, "It was very weird."

She tells me that she went to the police station in the morning, and they gave her Dickhead's number, making it clear that this was not some sort of revenge call. The goal was to get him to confess or at least corroborate facts to provide probable cause for a search warrant and potential arrest.

"I was a little confused," my mom goes on to say, "because they wanted me to call from my phone, which he would be able to see on caller ID."

My mom tried calling several times, but it went straight to voicemail. The officer then told her to text Dickhead, identifying herself and saying she needed to talk to him. He responded right away, saying that he was out but would be available to speak with her at 5:00 p.m. She came back to the police station that afternoon, but again he did not pick up when she called.

"We are driving back now," he texted her. The officer said it was better to talk when he was alone, so over text, Dickhead and my mom agreed to speak the next morning.

The next morning, she made the call from her office with the police listening in on the line.

This time, he answered. My mom tells me that at first, he was super friendly and they chitchatted about the winery he and his partner had visited the day before. She was nervous, so she let him talk, but then she came out with it: "You gave Alex piano lessons and drove him home from school."

Dickhead acknowledged that he had, but when my mom accused him of touching me inappropriately, he went silent for a moment. My mom continued telling him what I remembered. He didn't panic or even raise his voice, just stayed calm and denied everything.

It wasn't until she brought up him taking me to the park that his voice started rising.

"He said he'd only driven you home once, and that's when I knew for sure he was lying," my mom says. "I purposely asked him if he'd ever touched your brother, to see how he'd respond, and he quickly just said no. With you, though, he kept rambling on and on, saying that he didn't know where our deck was and that he'd never forced his way in."

My mom tells me that she kept pushing, hoping he would slip, but he never did. After about twenty minutes, when he could see that she wasn't going to drop it, he told her he had to go and hung up.

"So he didn't confess?" I finally say as much to myself as to her.

"No," my mom says. "I'm not entirely sure what happened since or what happens now. The officer texted that I did a great job right after the call, but I followed up and have not heard back from her."

I'm at a loss for words, still reeling that my mom had actually talked to Dickhead. But the more I think about it, the more I can see how poorly thought-out the whole thing had been—and the worse feeling I get about what will happen now.

"There was an entire twenty-four-hour gap between the first time you called him and when you actually talked to him?" I don't wait for her to say anything; I know the answer.

I pace around my apartment, gripping the phone harder, and my voice starts to rise. "This is the dumbest fucking thing I have ever heard in my life! You haven't spoken to him for over a decade, don't have his number, and call him totally out of the blue on the week between Christmas and New Year's. What did he think you were looking for, a fucking invoice?"

My mom says nothing.

"This is a sharp motherfucker, and he has been doing this for a long time. What is he going to say—'Yes, I did it. All my child porn is in the back closet there. Where are the cuffs?' How fucking stupid do they think he is? Did they even go in and search?"

This time I'm clearly looking for a response. "I think they went in yesterday afternoon," my mom says. "But I do think we would have heard if they'd found anything or made an arrest. You never know, though; I don't think you can predict what happens now."

"Un-fucking-believable," I say, shaking my head.

"This is just how they do it. It's definitely not over," my mom says. "We did get him to admit that he gave you lessons and drove you home." It sounds like she doesn't know what else to say and is grasping for any positives.

After a couple more minutes of sarcasm and anger, I tell her that I can't talk about this anymore.

"Okay. I love you. We are going to keep going here. I'll let you know if the police say anything."

I hang up without replying.

I feel a complete lack of control around the situation and just keep getting angrier. I go for a walk, hoping that will calm me down a bit, but I'm cussing under my breath and smacking my hands together the entire time. When I come back, I'm still fighting the urge to smash something.

# Splinter

n one of their best decisions, my parents sent me to prep school, where I had to wear a tie, for middle and high school. I spent much of those school years laughing in the hallways, brimming with energy, thankful both consciously and unconsciously for my new environment.

I was fortunate to make a bunch of good friends during this period. We all played sports together, pulled pranks on each other every day, went to breakfast before school, yelled at the volleyball games, and often spent weekend evenings looking for alcohol or weed. I felt welcomed by their families, sitting in their basements for hours, sometimes drinking but often just watching sports or playing video games.

However, as more than one friend told me, I could also be a real dick sometimes.

When a kid in my class, who was on the heavier side, poked gentle fun at my new shoes, I hit back that at least I wasn't a fat ass. In an argument with a teacher, I informed her that she was a moron. I said stuff like this regularly.

Even my jokes had a pointed edge to them. While I may have often been smiling, there was at times a sarcastic hostility beneath those grins.

The deeper anger would come out in flashes—when I slammed my helmet against a locker after we lost a football game or cussed up a storm after getting fouled on the pickup basketball court. After I got suspended once for losing a fist fight, my head of school correctly assessed I had a temper.

I was hurt enough on the inside that it was impossible for me not to project some of that pain outward.

The memories of what happened to me may have been gone, but

the feelings were still there, under the surface. They came out in the horrible haircuts, the ill-fitting clothing, and the way I didn't like to take my shirt off. In the tossing and turning at night. And how my butt got drenched in sweat when I was nervous.

I found myself obsessing for days, weeks, or longer about why I hadn't been invited to some party, why I hadn't played more in the basketball game, why a girl hadn't sat next to me in class, or nursing some other grudge that felt etched in my mind.

I also vigilantly assessed everyone around me. Sometimes I even heard a voice in my head pointing out what I perceived as weaknesses in them.

The night after two big exams and before the end-of-the-year track meet, my heart started racing as I was trying to go to bed. I never got to sleep. I chalked it up to being overscheduled and never thought about it again.

I was a decent student, but not great. One of my teachers joked I had a second semester senior attitude from the day I got there.

My locker looked like a crime scene. I was having enough trouble staying organized that I went to see a psychologist so I could qualify for school-based assistance. The summary concluded that I "demonstrated many of the organizational planning problems that are hallmarks of ADHD."

I started handing my keys and even my wallet to friends when we went out, not because I was drinking, but so I wouldn't lose them.

A part of me liked being social, especially if it meant getting out of my house. But there were other aspects of it that scared me.

On the way to a friend's for Thanksgiving drinks, I was already sweating. When I arrived to a crowded kitchen, I quickly got stuck in my nightmare. Some adult friend of my friend's family who I had never met would ask me how I knew the family. While I gave some bland response about going to school with my friend, I'd be worrying internally, *Is this person judging me? How can I get through this interaction in the fastest, least-awkward way possible so I can go downstairs and play beer pong?*

I particularly dreaded the moment there would be some sort of goodbye, whether it be a handshake or, god forbid, a hug. I tried to hold a drink in my hand so people were more likely to wave instead.

Friends observed that I didn't like adults or to be touched, and I joked back that I just preferred most people from a distance.

I knew something was different about me, but neither of my parents were known for their physical expressiveness, so I decided it made sense that I wasn't either.

As we got into high school, the conversation while we sat around someone's basement watching TV often turned to sex. The PG version involved one friend speculating what a girl in our class looked like naked and claiming she was into him. Another friend then reminisced about one of his successes amid a sea of failures. Someone else then confessed to the group that he had secretly hooked up with a girl under the stairs at Homecoming, only to discover that another one of our friends had also recently gotten with her.

I usually stayed silent during all of this, much to their confusion. Even if they were way more talk than actual action, my friends commented that I rarely got involved.

I didn't really think deeper about this. I simply attributed all these issues to the way I had been raised.

In 2003, my brother was diagnosed with severe autism. The doctor told my mom that he would never speak and may need to be institutionalized. She spent months crying.

In the years that followed, she had something akin to a religious conversion—not in personality but in priorities. All the energy she had once put into work was dedicated to getting him in a better spot. She never held a full-time corporate role again and spent most of her time at home with him and my sister.

It was hard not to notice the contrast with my early childhood, when she had been mostly absent.

I didn't feel much resentment toward my brother, who needed all the help he could get and was dissimilar enough from me to not be a good comparison point. I actually felt we were close, to the extent I was able to connect with him.

But I was unconsciously resentful of my sister, who was capable and still got the attention growing up that I had not.

Over the years, my brother made remarkable progress. But it came at a cost. My mom was stressed about him all the time, and it was a constant parade of therapists and special diets, with lots of money spent. At times they fought so loudly that it could be heard from anywhere in the house. Being around the two of them left me feeling on edge.

And even aside from his relationship with our mom, my brother was rigid and anxious about routines, needing to drive the same way home, listen to the exact same music in the car, or not turn off the TV until all the credits ended. He would have a meltdown if any of this did not happen.

So it was hard being at home. And when I was there, I never went into the piano room.

After getting frustrated with the public school district's inability to support my brother, my mom decided to start her own school for kids with learning challenges so he could go there. When she started working around the clock to get it up and running, we drifted even further apart.

My mom managed to get an enormous amount done. But she did it in a way that often made her not that fun to be around. She complained all the time, about things like a parent who had yelled at her, or someone, usually a teacher she had hired or my brother, not doing what they were supposed to be doing. It felt like a way for her to blow off steam, but I found it hard to relax around her.

I did not talk to her much directly during this period. When she did occasionally get more involved in my life, I was not always nice to her.

Those years also had plenty of friction with my dad, who started teaching math at my school the same year I got there. There were financial and logistical benefits to having us at the same campus, but I did not want him there.

We spent over an hour in the car driving to and from school each day. Sometimes we talked about sports or joked about school gossip. But often the rides turned into an interrogation about my grades, which he sometimes knew before me, or why I was not doing better in sports, or lectures about how I presented myself. Math, my biggest weakness, was a particular source of friction.

One day in high school, toward the end of the semester, my dad and I were walking out to the parking lot to head home when I ran into a friend. The following day was designated to study for exams, and school attendance was optional. The friend asked if I would be coming in tomorrow. I said no and that I thought showing up was a waste of time. My dad immediately interjected to tell me that was inappropriate. I fired right back that he should shut up and mind his own business. He spent the entire car ride home that day yelling that I should never tell him to shut up, especially where he worked.

He frequently started sentences with "You have to," or "You need," both of which I saw as ways for him to tell me what to do under the pretense of guidance. I found that every time I pushed back, he pushed harder, so I usually said nothing and resented him instead.

My dad's concerns about my grades or athletic performance seemed to have more to do with validating him as a parent and a person than anything to do with me. Positive reinforcement from him felt conditional on achievement. Spending so much time together did not bring us closer.

Our family's activities often revolved around my brother and sister. I started begging out of family vacations and for a time fantasized about going to boarding school.

The running joke among some of my friends when I ended up at their houses for different holidays was that I was there because I hated my family.

One day during my sophomore year of high school, I got a message from one of the guidance counselors, Mrs. Hill, asking to meet. I didn't know who she was, and my first and second thoughts were that I had said something that had offended someone and was in trouble.

I was nervous walking into her office, but to my surprise, she was cool, with a good sense of humor and a directness I appreciated. This was her first year as a counselor, and she was only a decade older than me.

She was surprisingly aware of the social dynamics at our school and seemed more like an older peer than some elderly lady up in the clouds.

When I got in there, I had no plans to talk about anything, but after a couple of minutes, it felt like a normal thing to do. It turned out that one of my teachers had concerns about how I was doing and asked Mrs. Hill to check in. She genuinely listened, and I remember feeling a tiny bit lighter after I left.

I saw her sporadically through the rest of high school as a sounding board to talk about how things were going.

Most of my teachers and coaches during this period came and went without too much thought. But several of them would have a lifelong positive impact because I could tell they cared about me.

Deep down, I was struggling even then. But because of the strong influences and support I had around me, I didn't do anything that dumb and made it through high school without too much damage. Those years were the one period of my life post-abuse when I was still open enough to trust people and felt connected to a larger community. It was the only period in my life when I had plenty of friends.

But at the time, things did not seem that great. I was desperate to move out and start fresh.

When it came time to pick a college, so many people around me were so neurotic about their options that I went the other way and chose not to put that much thought into it. I didn't know many people in college and never visited anyone on a campus, only going on some choreographed tours. Everything I knew about the experience came from pop culture.

I don't recall my parents offering much input on college. But even if they had, I wouldn't have listened.

I knew I wanted to go somewhere warm, was too intimidated to go to a big school, and had loved visiting California as a kid. Los Angeles felt like everything staid northern Virginia was not, so I decided to go to a private school there.

I lasted all of seven weeks. From the second I moved into a triple, I knew I had made a mistake. There was not much campus life, and I was a fish out of water in LA, especially without a car. The culture shock between me and the mostly Southern California-based student body was way bigger than I'd imagined.

But it was also the first time in a long time I had to meet new people. I hadn't grasped just how insular and insecure I had become over the intervening years, how uncomfortable and anxious I was in a new environment. I was miserable, and it was crystal clear I was not going to last there, so I decided to pull the plug early and withdraw.

Leaving was the right move for me, but when I got back to Virginia, I was a mess. It was the first time I had ever felt like I was off track. I had expectations about how the "best years of my life" were supposed to go, and while it was my own fault, I already felt like I had failed.

I spent the rest of my freshman year living at home, going to community college, and working construction. Although I could have no idea that years later, when my dick stopped working, I would have killed to be back in the position I was then, at the time it felt devastating.

Mrs. Hill and I stayed in touch after I graduated. When I returned to Virginia, she suggested I come see her to figure out how to best move forward. I was too embarrassed to show my face at my high school just months after I'd graduated, so she found somewhere off campus where we could meet.

I ended up seeing her every week the rest of that school year, for free.

It was more support than therapy. We were not reinventing the wheel in these sessions. "What is one positive thing that happened this week?" she'd ask me. Or "What can you do to make this time meaningful?"

But I was already struggling in ways I could not see and had no idea how to resolve. That was the year I could have easily slid into alcohol, drugs, or other negative behaviors. While it was still a shitty year, the biggest reason I never melted down was because of her support. I always felt like she believed in me and saw the best in me, even when I couldn't see it myself.

I transferred to a state school for sophomore year. As a transfer, it felt like I had already missed the boat on meeting people. I flirted with some social fraternities, but my friends from high school universally agreed I was not a frat guy, and I came to the same conclusion. I could have joined other groups, but I found myself getting bitter instead and spending much of that year reading books or holed up on my computer, wishing I was somewhere else.

I struggled to see the real-world applicability of many of the classes I was taking. Between the academic and social issues, I was not sure why I was there. I felt like a disillusioned outsider again, in much the same way I was during my early childhood.

By the time I got to college, some part of me knew I needed help, especially when I drank. But usually when those feelings came up, I just told myself to be tougher. By then, being normal and having had a decent childhood was an identity-driven belief that I struggled to see past most of the time. In part because I had grown up well off, I felt I had no reason to be unhappy. I wasn't sure what I would even claim to be a victim of.

Sometimes I would go to the counseling center. It is still not clear to me why I went. I think I was mostly just looking for someone to validate what I wanted to be true, that I was fine. But another part of me wanted to try to feel better without putting in any effort.

After a couple of sessions I could see it was kind of useless and told the counselors that I thought I had worked through things. They agreed that I had made great progress. It felt performative.

Even if I had wanted to change, the only two modalities I was aware of were talk therapy and antidepressants, one of which I was sort of already doing, the other unappealing for its physical side effects, because it seemed kind of drastic, and because I didn't want to be on a drug indefinitely.

I got into self-improvement instead. I started doing CrossFit several times a week and was in the best physical shape of my life. I switched to a high-protein diet. My sleep hygiene on nights I didn't drink was good. Everything was worse when any of these things got off track.

But even with these lifestyle changes, I was anxious, had a hard time sleeping, and often woke up feeling off.

"Let's go upstairs," she whispered.

I was standing in a huge living room full of people, Solo cup in hand, at a party for my gym. It was crowded enough that I hadn't noticed a tall, hot, blond girl—who I occasionally did CrossFit with but didn't know at all—come up and whisper into my right ear. I'm deaf in that ear, so I repositioned myself to face her.

"What?"

"Let's go upstairs," she said again, face flushed.

"To do shots?" I asked, confused. We'd never spoken or even really acknowledged each other, although I'd heard her talk about her older boyfriend. I'd even seen him pick her up from class once or twice.

"No, let's hook up upstairs," she said, grabbing my hand. I was pretty drunk at this point, but not enough not to be stunned, especially because I considered her out of my league.

She started dancing up against me, and I smiled awkwardly. "Don't you have a boyfriend?"

"Yeah," she replied shortly. She let go of my hand, and I could tell she was a little surprised where the conversation had gone.

After thirty seconds of us just staring at each other, I told her I had to get another drink and then left the party because I was "too drunk." I occasionally saw her after that, and we went right back to not acknowledging each other.

Another night, during one of my last semesters in college, I was hammered and ambling around a crowded bar with one of my only friends on campus when someone bear-hugged me from behind. When I turned around to see who it was, I was stunned. It was a girl

I didn't know well but had had a crush on for a while. We'd spoken once at a potluck/interview event for a business fraternity I'd joined the previous semester. She and I had hit it off, having grown up near each other and gone to similar high schools. We even had friends of friends in common.

I'd felt a spark, even telling a roommate about it when I got home. The fraternity was big and didn't have many events, but I went to most of them in hopes that she would be there. By the time that school year had ended, I hadn't spoken to her again, and I was too scared to reach out, out of the blue.

This semester she had a class in the same building as I did, and sometimes I'd see her leaving as I was walking in. I was still not even sure she remembered who I was. Until this bear hug.

"Hey!" she said with the biggest drunken grin on her face, still hugging me as tight as she could. I was too drunk to remember exactly what we talked about, but I do know we laughed for a while, and I think we found a table to sit at. One of the last things I remember before completely blacking out was leaving her for a second, saying I had to go to the bathroom, but actually going up to the crowded bar area and ordering and downing several more shots for myself.

The next morning, I woke up bleary eyed and thought we might have made out but didn't really know.

After that, it felt like I ran into her everywhere—in hallways, around campus, or at fraternity meetings. I could tell she wanted me to come up and talk to her, but every time I saw her, I froze up, barely able to give a small wave before turning away or looking down at the ground. I kept hoping to run into her at a bar again, when I was drunk and feeling good, but it never happened. As I kept running into her but never made a move, I could see her giving up on me in what I assumed was disgust.

I wanted to believe I was a courageous person but instead every time I ran into her and for years afterward, I ruminated that I was coward.

I'd always had a bunch of issues around sex, but it became more apparent during my college years. I struggled with everything other than getting it up, terrified of both physical and emotional intimacy. I was concerned about coming off as creepy, which I associated with any expression of interest. I had all sorts of performance anxiety, particularly as I got older and it was assumed I'd already had some experience.

I am not a virgin, but not far off. I've never had sex sober in my life, and I can count on one hand the number of times I've had sex where I wasn't raped.

I had been rejected a couple of times in high school, but by the time I got to college, I rarely got rejected anymore—mainly because I was too scared to put myself out there in any way, especially when I was sober. I took a perverse sense of pride in not seeming interested because it made it impossible for me to get hurt.

But I looked for rejection everywhere and was devastated at even the slightest hint of it. When it did happen, I would immediately spiral about why girls did not like me. The second anyone actually showed interest, however, I couldn't run away fast enough. I would make excuses, drink to the point of belligerence, leave the bar, or find other ways to self-sabotage. I once spent five days at the house of a girl I liked without making any sort of move. By the end, I could feel frustration radiating off her in a way that made me loathe myself.

After instances like that, the blame would start. I would blame my parents or blame myself.

It was almost impossible for me to imagine a girl I liked also liking me. There was a part of me that believed that either having a girlfriend or hooking up with a bunch of girls would make these negative feelings about myself and being a man go away. Not having any sex certainly wasn't working.

I could feel judgment from friends and my dad about why I didn't have a girlfriend or seem to be having sex. Some of my friends and several girls speculated I was gay. It hurt because I knew I wasn't.

But when I did occasionally manage to get myself into an intimate situation, I felt detached, almost zoned out, like I was observing rather than participating.

I don't think I ever had a porn problem. Porn never kept me from doing other things I wanted to do. But I watched it every day in those years.

I only ever drank alcohol socially. Even at my peak, I was only drinking two or three nights a week. In the summers, I would sometimes go weeks or even months barely touching it.

But I had a hard time stopping once I got started, sometimes after a couple of drinks almost demanding to keep the booze flowing. The amount I needed to drink to get the negative voice in my head to go away meant that three drinks turned into ten very quickly. I liked me better when I was drunk, and as far as I could tell, so did everyone else. I felt especially uncomfortable around big groups of people or in places where physical intimacy was a possibility, even an expectation. So while I often had fun drinking, I frequently overdid it and had to talk my way out of several alcohol citations, one while driving.

While I was in college, my dad was diagnosed with pancreatic cancer. The prognosis was very poor. It looked like he would die soon. It was rough on everyone. But after the first couple of weeks, I felt mostly numb to it.

Some of that numbness was personal. My dad's diagnosis felt like the culmination of our relationship going south. But it also showed how much like a robot I had become and my inability to feel sadness or other deep emotions for myself or anyone else.

My dad was young and otherwise in good physical health when they caught it early. After almost twenty rounds of chemotherapy, he had most of his pancreas removed. (Nine years post-diagnosis, thankfully, he is still alive.) But for me, his diagnosis and the aftermath highlighted how broken I felt inside.

After a year at my second college, I decided I didn't want to be there. Instead, I studied abroad, attempting to run away from my problems.

I had not traveled much internationally before. At the beginning, going abroad was great for me. London felt expansive and exciting a in a way northern Virginia and my college town did not. I had fewer expectations and less self-judgment in places where no one knew me. After spending a couple of years feeling confined and sulking, traveling showed me that there was a bigger world out there—and it gave me confidence to navigate that world. My first study abroad encouraged me to join more things when I got back to my campus, even if none of them really stuck.

To their credit, my parents were supportive of these trips. I ended up studying abroad several times over the second half of college, even taking an extra year to graduate so I could go again. For a while, travel made everything better.

But over time, anxiety started creeping back in. No matter how far away I went, my issues came with me.

It was the summer after I graduated, running myself ragged, that I had my ill-fated bike ride.

I really started paying the price for my childhood in college. There was a constant inability to relax, trust issues, a major self-esteem problem, trouble feeling deep emotions like joy or sadness, combined with drinking too much alcohol.

I was mad enough about how it went that, in a rage, I drunkenly tossed my laptop over my balcony and into the woods below on one of the last nights I was at my campus. I didn't attend my graduation both because I was abroad and because I knew I wouldn't have any friends there. By the time I left, I felt unrecognizable to my high school self.

The rapes were like an infected splinter—the longer they went unaddressed, the worse things got, until that sliver of wood eventually worked its way to the surface in the form of all my pelvic issues. My college years began a long, isolating decade that I am still unwinding.

# Psilocybin

A few weeks after I go to the police, it's time for psilocybin. Katrina had warned that mushrooms can get dark, that it was important for me to be careful and work my way up to higher doses. So in my previous session I had done the typical dose of MDMA but combined it with two grams of psilocybin. It was hard but didn't feel much different than the session before.

This time, however, the plan is to go up to four grams with no MDMA.

In the days leading up to the session, I feel a dark and looming sense of dread at the thought of doing that many mushrooms.

It's only after my first psilocybin journey that I start consciously struggling with shame. I have already been feeling plenty of fear and anger, but until psilocybin I hadn't felt shame or even considered shame as a concept much at all. How I perceived myself and my behavior seemed natural to me. My thoughts and who I was at my core felt the same.

But after even one mushroom session, I begin to realize what I had once seen as normal self-perception is actually a deep and almost overwhelming sense of embarrassment and self-disapproval. Not only do I have shame; I have a crippling amount of it.

I constantly replay even the smallest negative interactions in my head, ruminating about decisions I screwed up in the past, worried that what I said came out wrong, anxious that whatever I happened to be doing at the time was not right.

I quickly recognize that these negative thought patterns all lead to the same conclusion: that deep down I am a bad person and always will be. These patterns of self-loathing had been there for a long time, but before psilocybin I could not see them.

Even after I start getting occasional glimpses outside of these negative self-beliefs, they seem impossible to stop or change. They feel deeply ingrained, like my default setting, as if they are a permanent part of me.

The worst thought pattern in the days leading up to the session is the panic wondering if I had raped children, just like Dickhead. My logic is that if I had repressed being abused, I could have also repressed being an abuser. It doesn't have any grounding in reality, and sometimes I can see so clearly that it is bullshit. Other times, however, I can't shake the fear.

I am terrified that me being a child molester or some other horrible thing will come up in a session and Katrina will be so appalled that she'll leave me alone in the room. My mom will grasp for something positive to cling to, but she'll be too stunned to know what to say.

I come to see that these shame-based fears that those closest to me would abandon me and not love me anymore were remarkably similar to what seven-year-old me thought would happen if I told people that Dickhead was touching me inappropriately.

I am silent on the drive over to Katrina's. We are in her room, going over how much I'm going to take and what's going to happen today, when I start crying. I tell her I'm scared of the mushrooms and not sure I can do it. I start pacing around in a panic, hands on my head. We take Chester for a quick walk around the block to try to get me to calm down.

Katrina is composed. She tells me we don't have to do anything I don't want to do, and she is fine canceling. But she adds that she thinks the mushrooms are a good next step in my healing journey if I am up for it—that I've already made it through the hardest part, and now it's about reorganizing my psyche. And, to her, it seemed like the two grams last session went well.

We decide I will start with a half dose of MDMA and two grams of psilocybin, and if I am feeling up for it, I can take the other two grams in an hour or so.

The MDMA comes on first. I read that if I listened closely, the medicine would tell me when I was done with it. That sounded strange to me, but I also kept hoping I would get some sort of message that it was time to move on from MDMA. Even after six sessions, however, I still don't feel ready to move forward.

I have known for a while that the abuse ended with Dickhead choking me unconscious.

But during this MDMA session, I look at him breaking into my house for the first time on medicine. No one home and me pacing with the phone in my hand. Watching Dickhead pull up the driveway. The rage in his eyes as he barreled through my kitchen, the way he clocked me from behind, and how my arms flailed as he suffocated me. I verbalize all this out loud to Katrina while my body shakes like a leaf.

I realize part of the reason I was panicking so badly was that I was not ready for the mushrooms alone today.

But after I go through the final confrontation with Dickhead, I get the message that it's time to move on from MDMA, that all the big stuff with him has come up, and that to do any more, at least right now, would set me back.

After an hour, I decide to take the second two grams of mushrooms. The MDMA starts to fade, and the mushrooms come on stronger.

Things begin to feel darker and darker. It feels like my mind is expanding, like I am seeing beyond myself in a way I never have before.

I realize that whatever is happening on this planet is both incomprehensibly large and has been going on for a very long time. That I am just passing through for what feels like a split second. And how impermanent, even fleeting, my existence is.

I start to feel smaller than I have ever felt. Like I am nothing more than a speck of dust in the wind or the tiniest of ants looking up at the world. It hurts my brain to feel so meaningless. I struggle to process it.

Already reeling, it occurs to me that an unfathomable amount of life has already come and gone. And that I will die too. I see how close I've come to death already. Dying no longer feels far away; it *will* happen, even if I do everything right. And it could happen soon—the other shoe could drop for me at any moment.

When I think of myself dying, there is no connection to something bigger. I see nothing beyond a fade to black.

Before I started psychedelics, dying felt almost hypothetical, something I had never truly considered. But today the inevitably of death, the possibility of it happening at any moment, and my terror around what will happen when it does is front and center, like a flashing billboard in the dark. I realize the reason I struggled to see how truly small I am and consider my death before today is because it is so painful to my ego.

This whole time, I feel more emotion than I can ever remember feeling. Like I have woken up from a long nap of being unable to feel.

But it hurts. I see why I couldn't feel some of the deep emotions before. Not being able to cry or feel sadness is better than this.

Just as I am starting to break down, I see Mrs. Hill and two close friends. They seem so light in a way I couldn't see before. When I think about them, I feel, at least for a split second, a sense of deep love and connectedness.

And then the feelings of a broader world leave, and I start razor focusing on myself.

I try not to think about them. I try to think about anything else. But I have little control on this dosage of mushrooms.

Dickhead and Fuckhead appear in my consciousness. They feel so big, towering over me, circling me as I sit in the backseat of that car. I relive them shouting at each other while I am covered in blood. I am eight years old again, and all I can see is Fuckhead reaching for me in the backseat.

I start screaming and have to take the mask off in a panic, breathing heavily, still too high to get up.

"Katrina," I say in a soft voice. She is only feet away, but she comes closer and holds my hand. I whisper, "They really got me."

Katrina hesitates for a second, seeming to decide what to say. Finally, she says, "They did get you. They absolutely got you."

I have known for months what happened. But before, even in talking about it out loud, there had been little emotion around it. I felt disconnected from it, like I was talking about it happening to someone else. I even cracked some dark jokes about it to Katrina.

But today with the mushrooms, it hits me in a deep and visceral way that this horrible thing happened not to someone else, but to me.

I see myself struggling to breathe on my bed after it happened, and for the first time, I feel connected to how painful it was and how much I suffered in the aftermath. How close I came to killing myself in the days after. That a part of me died that day.

"I get so mad, but actually I am so sad," I say, only now discovering this truth. For the first time on psychedelics, I start to cry.

"Why did this happen to me?" I ask Katrina in a voice that sounds more like a kid than an adult. She sighs in a sympathetic way and says she doesn't know. But at this point, it unfortunately doesn't matter.

"Am I going to be okay?" I ask, my voice still a whisper.

She hesitates again. "Probably not tomorrow or next month, but I do think over time you can heal."

"I don't want to be broken," I say.

"You are not broken," Katrina replies. "There will always be scars, though."

The moment feels beyond words, and we continue to hold hands as the soft music plays in the background, my brain going quiet, like a group of animals with their heads down in mourning, slow tears streaming down my cheeks.

As the session winds down fully, I know I'm in trouble. I'm having suicidal thoughts even before I take the mask off. I say out loud, more to myself than Katrina, "I don't want to be alive right now."

It is pitch black on the walk around the block, one of the rare winter nights in Austin when I can see my breath. I can hear the emptiness, the lifelessness in my own voice, very much in my own thoughts, not listening to my mom or Katrina.

I have never struggled with conscious depression before. I've always had plenty of anxiety, but getting up and moving have never been hard for me.

In the days and weeks after my first big session with psilocybin, however, I struggle to get out of bed.

Sometimes I feel calm, but I have no energy. Ideas of suicide are constantly running through the back of my mind, and sometimes they are very loud. Life feels heavy and grim, bleak and dangerous. I struggle to see my way out, unable to imagine a time when I will not feel as despondent as I do now.

I can't hear about bad things happening to someone else without going into a full-blown panic that something similar will happen to me. Food doesn't taste good. The book I'm reading suddenly seems pointless.

*Nothing matters*, I reason. *In the long run, we are all dead anyway.*

If the second session of MDMA was the high point of my anxiety, the second time I did psilocybin was the high point of my depression—and my lowest point of all.

I can tell my mom is concerned by how listless I am. She stays with me the whole next week.

In my integration session, Katrina is as concerned as I've ever seen her. "We could try taking a break. We could try a mood stabilizer. No one wants to lose you. That is the most important thing right now."

I tell her I will be fine. Even I'm unconvinced.

"You've been through a lot," Katrina says. "In some ways, I'd be more perplexed if you weren't having a hard time. All psychedelics do is hold a mirror up back to you. Bad trips like the one you had don't just come out of nowhere; they come from somewhere inside."

"I feel small and meaningless," I say.

"I don't agree with meaningless, but the feeling of smallness is an important part of the experience. Everyone is self-centered to some degree, and children are very self-centered before growing out of it. People with childhood trauma tend to get stuck in that egotistical phase as an adaptive response to being hurt, which ultimately leads to suffering. Psychedelics are maybe the only thing that, in the right circumstances, can truly break through and help people see there is more to life than just them and their suffering. It can be very painful, though."

"I can't stop thinking about death," I reply.

"Well, you will die," Katrina says. "And I'd be lying if I said you have total control over when or how it is going to happen. Where I like to go with that is how will you make meaning with the finite time you are here, in this body? And if you develop a spiritual practice, you might consider what exactly is death anyway? Your ego dies; your body dies, but does all of you die?"

Katrina and my mom check in on me almost every morning. I have to beg off my mom trying to visit every weekend. At times I am quite concerned about myself, but I never feel I am truly in danger.

I also don't want to go on a drug regimen, check myself in anywhere, or have my mom or anyone else come live with me.

I am determined to get through this. I have gotten myself this far, so I can't stumble now. I know from experience that as I get further away from the session, as I reset myself, things tend to get a little better.

I feel the worst when I am alone, sitting still in my apartment, especially when it's dark outside, so I do my best to rarely put myself in that situation. I walk all around Austin, getting in twenty-five to thirty thousand steps every day, in the sunlight, sometimes to different food trucks, but more often just to be out in nature.

Austin is certainly not perfect, but I will always be grateful for the city's mild winters, friendly people, relaxed vibe, and emphasis on wellness—even if sometimes it gets a little crazy.

I find meeting new people hard during this period, so I lean on old friends, many of whom come to visit.

And when walking doesn't work, or on weekends when I don't have friends around, I drive.

I roam all over Texas—and after I run out of places in Texas, I go farther, venturing all over the South on weekend trips.

It doesn't matter where I go as long as I haven't been there before. I pick somewhere on Thursday night, come up with a list of things I want to see and places to eat, make plenty of stops on the way, walk around for a couple of hours, and then move on somewhere else.

The drive is often the best part. I feel a sense of peace being in motion that I don't feel when I'm standing still. Having a clear destination and something other than the rapes to concentrate on helps take my mind off how awful I feel.

Between the trips, friend visits, working with Katrina, and readjusting from the session, things slowly begin to lift out of the danger zone over the next couple of months.

And of course, right as I'm feeling a little better, I decide it's time to push the envelope.

# The Letter

On January 11, 2022, my mom speaks to the police officer for the first time since doing the control call. The officer tells her that they did not find anything incriminating in his apartment, that she could not make him take a polygraph, and for the police to try to find other victims or interview anyone else would constitute harassment. She adds that anyone else coming forward would have no impact on my case anyway.

At one point, the officer indicates that she thinks I'm too emotional to testify, which I find frustrating because if I had not been emotional, I suspect that would have been used against me as well, in the "if this really happened, why are you not more upset?" vein.

The officer says someone from my school system will be reaching out soon, but she is unable to provide contact information for anyone there.

It becomes clear that the police are not going to do anything further on this. Even before I went to the police, I didn't think I alone could put Dickhead in jail—but I did believe I could get him out of a school and start the process of holding him accountable.

I assume that once the school district gets wind of my allegations, especially knowing they are coming from a male, they will find a way to get him out of there. I don't expect them to investigate because nothing that could come out of an investigation would make the school district look good. I don't even expect them to reach out to me, let alone apologize.

But if someone else comes forward, even years later, and it ever comes out that someone had already made an accusation to the police, it could make the school district look bad. I believe the liability of keeping him around kids outweighs the risk for them of letting him go.

I figure they'll likely find a way to put him on some sort of paid leave, shuffle some paper around to mitigate liability, not renew his contract, and take the chance of an accused child molester suing them.

This does not happen.

A week after I went to the police, my mom's assistant called Dickhead's school and asked to speak with him. They patched her right through. She tried again a month later, and the same thing happened. After that, my mom emailed the school district's head of legal and Dickhead's principal for a status update on their investigation. There was no reply.

It became clear that they were going to close the case, and Dickhead would be able to move on unscathed, like nothing had ever happened.

At this point, my mom and I are pissed. My mom talks to several lawyers who are conservative and not helpful regarding next steps. There's no protocol about what to do now.

But even before I'd gone to the police, I already had an idea.

I believe the people most likely to care whether their kids are going to school with a sexual predator are the parents of the children at Dickhead's school and maybe some of his coworkers. So I find the email addresses for Dickhead's parent-teacher association on his school's website and decide to write them directly.

I think a couple of things could happen once I send my email. Public pressure might force the police to revisit the case, so I'm careful not to antagonize them in the letter, even though I'm frustrated regarding their lack of effort. The letter could spread and potentially encourage others to come forward. I also know Dickhead will read it, and sending it will be therapeutic. Finally, I don't think there's any way he can continue working in a school once I send it.

I decide the only way I could ever regret sending the letter is if I'm not absolutely certain it was him. But I've never been more certain of anything in my life—so there's no way sending it will be a mistake.

I purposely tell my male survivor group and all my practitioners I am going to send it, knowing that once I start telling people, it will be hard to walk back.

I set a date to send my letter, a Sunday in March. When the day arrives, my mom and I are on the phone reading through it, scrutinizing every sentence. Dickhead's email address is on the school website, and the only time my mom and I get in an argument is when I tell her I want to copy him on the letter. She puts her foot down on that one, and I eventually relent.

The letter (which can be found in its entirety, with only some identifying information removed, in Appendix B) names Dickhead as someone who repeatedly raped me during first and second grades, both in and out of school. There are thirty-two people copied on the email—the entire PTA for Dickhead's current school, the entire

PTA for his and my former elementary school, principals for both schools, members of the school board, the superintendent, as well as several of his underlings. The subject line is "Notification of Sexual Abuse."

I'm mad enough about everything that happened that I don't feel much fear about sending it.

"It has to be your decision," my mom says as we're saying goodbye. "But I support you to the moon and back."

I hang up with her and hit send.

I'm alone and don't know what to do with myself after sending it. It feels surreal, like a weight has been lifted off my shoulders.

My mom and Katrina both text encouragement. But now that it has been sent, the fear starts to come through in a way it hadn't before. I don't call anyone, celebrate, cry, or anything like that. Instead, I go for a long walk around Austin, eat a greasy cheeseburger, and try unsuccessfully to go to bed early. As I drift off to sleep, I think, *I did it.*

And when I think about it later, sending that letter is one of the proudest moments of my life.

I don't want to see any responses to the letter, so I have my mom check the email address I created to send it. I even have her change the password so I'm not tempted to check. I tell her not to contact me about it unless something is needed.

The days drag by. My mom doesn't volunteer anything, and I'm too afraid to ask.

Finally, I break down and call her. Before I can even say hello, she says, "This isn't over unless you want it to be over."

That's when I know it had not gone well.

On the Tuesday morning after I sent the letter, and after months of little to no response, the officer in charge of my case reached out saying she needed to speak to my mom. The last time they had communicated, the police had not yet picked a prosecutor. On the phone, the officer informed my mom that not only had they chosen a prosecutor, but he had declined prosecution that morning. She said that the search warrant had not turned up evidence, and the emails from the school system had been lost in a system upgrade.

She explained that the commonwealth attorney did not think they could get a conviction. She said that one of the attorney's arguments was that "At this time, he is not certain that we have enough to say it was Dickhead," and the attorney was concerned that I "had this experience with someone else and now was fixated on Dickhead."

The officer ended the call by saying, "With our cases and our caseloads that we have, we, unfortunately, are used to the fact that in some cases we don't have accountability for some things that we know to have happened."

Hours after that call, the assistant superintendent had responded to my letter and copied the superintendent:

Alex,

Good afternoon. We have received the concerns you sent about a School System staff member. We have coordinated closely with the County Police Department, who have investigated your allegations. The police and the Commonwealth Attorney's Office have now decided to close the investigation and do not intend to bring charges.

The School System also does not have any basis to take further action at this time. Please contact me if you have any questions or would like to discuss.

I chose not to reply. It is still the only response I have ever received to the letter.

The next morning, a friend of my mom's forwarded her the following email, which went out to parents of my elementary school:

Dear Families,

We are aware that some in our community have received concerns about a former staff member. The School System Human Resources Department coordinated closely with the County Police Department, who investigated the concerns. The police and the Commonwealth Attorney's Office have now decided to close the investigation and do not intend to bring charges. The School System is satisfied that the police looked into this matter thoroughly and also considers it closed. Please contact me if you have any questions or concerns.

Signed,

The Current Principal

I'm silent as my mom tells me all of this. It's a tough call, to put it mildly.

"We are on the right side here. It is just not going to happen overnight," she says.

I tell her I have to go.

In the days that follow, I hear rumors of a tense PTA meeting at Dickhead's current school—that his principal said there was no evidence, I must have been mistaken or had some kind of mental health issue, she knew Dickhead's character, and he had her full support.

After that, I'm even more determined not to let this go, so my mom and I start interviewing lawyers about what happened and what to do next.

One lawyer tells us, "Everyone knows they should hire a lawyer when they get accused of a crime, and they should. But they should also hire a lawyer if they are accusing someone of a crime like yours. The reality is the police have wide discretion in how they want to approach these things. While they may smile and try to make it seem like they are your friend, they are not. They *always* have their own agenda that may or may not align with yours, even as a victim.

"If you don't have someone directly advocating for you, making sure the police are doing what they are supposed to be doing, you never really know. If they don't think the prosecutor's office is likely to do anything with the case, or it might require real work that they don't want to do, you are shit out of luck. They don't make that much. They hate paperwork. They have a bunch of cases to work on, and they get paid the same no matter how much effort they put in."

It sinks in that I have fucked up here both in not hiring a lawyer and in expecting the police to do much to generate evidence.

If Dickhead ever responded to my letter, I did not hear about it. He definitely did not sue me.

A few months after the case is closed, I discover that Dickhead received the Outstanding School-Based Professional Employee of the Year award from his school for the 2021–22 school year.

# Not Personal

I n the weeks after my letter is dismissed, it's time for another mushroom session, my first without MDMA.

I decide to keep going with the psychedelics because I know what life looks like without them, and I have already noticed a distinct decline in day-to-day anger since I started doing psilocybin.

Depression has replaced some of that anger, but I also have less emotional reactivity. Bad traffic or things at work that used to make me mad no longer seem worth getting upset about.

But most importantly, I decide that if I'm going to be alive, I might as well try to heal. Right now, it feels like psychedelics are the best way for me to do that.

Before the session begins, I tell Katrina I am in a fight with Dickhead and my school system and that no matter how long it takes, I am going to win.

And then the mushrooms start coming on. It's like a bad dream I can't escape from.

It is not new memories so much as painful emotions. Every negative thought pattern of fear, of shame, of self-loathing feels like it is being amplified in a way I did not know was possible. It's like my brain is on fire. I start screaming, "I want to die!" over and over again at the top of my lungs. I can't think about anything else, the emotional agony coming on like tidal waves.

The eye mask makes things worse; I feel trapped in my own mind.

I'll do anything to make this stop. I scream at Katrina, demanding a gun so I can kill myself. I yell for the MDMA, knowing it will soften whatever is going on right now and make some of these terrible feelings go away.

Katrina tells me that it's not time yet and she thinks I can go longer with the mushrooms. These are feelings I suppressed when I was little, and now it's time to let them go.

I yell the meanest things I have ever said about my mom, my dad, and my second-grade teacher.

But as I begin to peak on the mushrooms, I stop talking about them and start talking about me.

"I don't want to be here, and I hate being alive."

"All I am and ever will be is someone who got a raped a lot."

"Those motherfuckers should have just murdered me and saved us all the trouble."

"I am a freak, just like he said."

A part of me can't believe what is coming out of my mouth. But it feels very real.

I shout that I want to quit psychedelics for good and I hate mushrooms.

At one point, I decide I can't handle this, take off the mask for a second, and try to get up off the bed. Everything is moving, and my head is still on fire, so I put the mask back on, just along for the ride now.

I scream over and over again, "I am a failure!"

I am stuck in the loop of this negative thought pattern, unable to think about anything else or get myself out of it.

And then, in the middle of window-shaking screams, Katrina interrupts to ask how my pelvis is doing now.

"The same as it fucking was twenty minutes ago!" I yell. "It's never enough with you. You're always dumping expectations on people."

"That is not something I do, Alex," Katrina says sternly, her voice suddenly intensifying. "I have not set any expectations around your healing; *you* have been doing that since the second you walked in here."

"You're always judging me. There's always something I'm not doing right, something I'm not saying. And now you are getting angry, which tells me I'm onto something!" I scream over the soft music, even though we are just feet away from each other.

"I'm getting frustrated because you are attributing negative beliefs you have about yourself onto me, and that is not fair," Katrina says.

"I don't want to end up like you, childless and alone!"

"I have never said you should live like me!" Katrina is louder now. "Again, I think you are projecting your own fears around being judged and intimacy as a way to push me away."

I am struggling to make sense. The mushrooms interfere with my ability to get the words out. But I yell more than once, "We can't work together anymore, and we are fucking *done*."

Then I go right back to screaming, "I want to die!" at the top of my lungs. It's coming up from somewhere deep inside me, some place I did not know was there until today. Even Chester licking me can't get me out of it.

In some ways, I have never felt more alive, vibrating to every chord of the music in the background. This feels like my truth. It is all coming out now.

At the four-hour mark, Katrina finally hands me some MDMA to try to calm me down, almost insisting that I take it. I fight with her about this, too, some part of me wanting to continue emoting, before I eventually give in.

As the MDMA kicks in, I start coming down and begin speaking in complete sentences again. I tell Katrina I don't think it is a good idea for us to work together anymore, that I need someone with more experience and who I am more comfortable with.

Katrina sighs. "You are free to do what you want, but I think you are going to run into the exact same issues with someone else."

"I don't understand why you can't just wish me well," I snark back. "I thought shamans weren't attached to the outcome."

"I'm human, Alex. I am doing my best to not take any of this personally, but you are trying very hard to make it personal. And I do care. But if you feel you would be better served elsewhere and want to move on, so be it." Katrina is now scribbling something down on a piece of paper and says this last part without even looking up at me.

We spend most the rest of the wind-down in silence. When my mom arrives, she does most of the talking on the awkward walk around the block. Katrina and I do not make eye contact with her or each other, neither of us giving more than an occasional grunt.

On the way home, I tell my mom that I'm not sure Katrina and I will keep working together.

My mom is quiet for a second before saying, "I'll support you whatever you decide. And I know things are still very hard, especially on weeks you do this. But it could be good to remember how bad things were—it was like watching a slow-motion car crash. You were mad all the time, yelling at me, yelling at the doctors, panicking about your body. I had no idea what to do to help you. I'm still worried and frustrated about everything, but I also see plenty of improvement. You are much less angry these days, less anxious, and you seem to have a much better understanding of yourself.

"I am still learning the best ways to support you, but I do think she knows how to help you. I was even thinking I might go see her."

We pull into my apartment, and I lie down on my couch, staring into space, still dazed, when for the first time all day, tears start flowing over how rough today was. The words come spilling out: "I don't want to be here. They hated me so much."

My mom starts speaking softly. "It is the biggest failure of my life that I was not there for you on this. But I do love you more than anything, and I am going to do whatever I can to help get you through it."

"I know," I say back.

"Of course, it brings me a ton of guilt that you have to be that way, but that doesn't mean for a second that I am not also proud of how strong you are…so proud. And it does seem like you have the right tools and people in place to get yourself through this and go on to live a great life."

I keep my integration session with Katrina. We start in a tense silence, not making much eye contact. I eventually mumble an apology for how the session went, which she accepts.

"It is important for you to feel that you can let it all out when you are in an open state like that," she says. "But even after you came out of it, you were still pretty harsh, so thank you. I do not think it is healthy to let you project your stuff on to me, but I wish I had been calmer about pushing back. I am certainly not perfect."

She continues, "I don't think you were any harder on me in there than you are on yourself. So while I was hurt, I ended up feeling a deep empathy for you around all this. It is always both of our responsibilities to communicate how we are feeling and to decide if we want to continue together. I journaled about it and I would like to keep working with you. So if you want to leave, it will be your choice."

"I don't want to work with someone else," I say in response, still mostly looking at my shoes.

She smiles. "Well, there is a ringing endorsement."

We move on to how rough the session was otherwise. She asks, "Have you ever articulated out loud that you wanted to die before?"

I tell her I have not.

"Setting aside your dick not working, how do you think a romantic relationship would have gone, knowing there was so much baggage under there?"

"Not well," I reply.

"You are not a failure, but that is where you are stuck right now. Because being hard on yourself, trying to be perfect, was a coping mechanism you used to get yourself through this. But perfection doesn't exist. It is a construct. And as you found out the hard way, the shadow is a real thing. How you or anyone else feels about themselves, at a deep and unconscious level, drives decision-making, what relationships people choose to be in, all of it.

"It is very hard for someone to love someone else more than they love themselves or to live a happy life if deep down, they do not believe they deserve it."

I'm silent, listening, as she continues. "Bringing those feelings to the surface is painful at first. But once you bring them up, you start working through them and build a new internal narrative for yourself—one based on love and acceptance, not judgment and self-loathing."

She goes on, "The emotional pain you are working through right now is real. But if all of you had wanted to die, you would not be here. All 'I want to die' really is, is a thought pattern arising from emotions like shame or feeling violated. Thoughts have no charge behind them. Unlike emotions, you have control over your thoughts; you can decide that you are not going to think those thoughts anymore.

"I think you still have some screams left to go, but soon I am going to start pushing back, asking if dying is what you really want. Or do you just want the emotional pain to go away? Because the pain will stop. I promise. Dying is permanent, though."

The next session, I scream, "I want to die," the entire time again. But I do not fight with Katrina, and at least in her telling, I do not shout quite as loud or as long as before.

"Do people think guys make up stories about sucking another man's dick or being raped for fun?"

I am sitting in Katrina's chair in the months after my letter was dismissed, still mad and unsure of what to do next. "I don't have him confused with the plumber. My letter doesn't seem to have circulated anywhere," I add bitterly.

"I get that you're hurt," Katrina says. "But I think it speaks to his smoothness and how he has been able to survive in that environment for so long. And I imagine it is scary to think that your child might not be safe at school or that someone you work with every day is not who they say they are. It is much easier to decide you are delusional and move on.

"You have the right to be angry if you want. But just like with him, I think you are going to drive yourself crazy if you take this personally. Often the deepest wounds people carry as adults are repeats of things that happened as children—not being heard, feeling like no one cares, having your reality questioned. Unfortunately, those are old stories for you.

"And you keep saying that you weren't believed, but you have no idea whether you were believed or not. If your school system felt you had no credibility, why did they take the time to put out a statement dismissing you? To me, you told people a story they didn't want to hear, and they choose not to take action. We are not there yet, but eventually you are going to get to a place where you see how much control you have over your reality and that almost everything in life, including how you decide to perceive this situation, is a choice."

"I would send the letter again," I say stubbornly.

"I know," Katrina says with a smile. "You will always be able to make this about you if you want. In my view, it is never personal, but just because it is not personal doesn't mean you can't enforce boundaries. You don't ever have to engage with Dickhead or the recipients of your letter again if you don't want to.

"But it doesn't come from a healed place to make someone listen or shame them into taking action. To fight him or your school system with anger puts you on their level, right in the muck with them.

Over time, I believe you can transcend them, rise above them, tell your story and continue to push for justice but do it from a higher place without all the anger and the vengeance.

"I do think it is also good to remember that holding him accountable won't change your healing trajectory. That is not to say it isn't worth doing. But doing the work, learning to love and accept yourself, that comes from in here," she says, pointing to her heart.

At first, I do not want to forgive Dickhead. In an argument with Katrina, I am annoyed enough that I look up the word forgiveness in the dictionary. "To stop feeling angry or resentful to someone for an offense, flaw or mistake."

"You don't ever have to forgive him," Katrina says, "But it would be a big step forward if you choose to. It is not about excusing what happened but about letting go of negative feelings and anger, not out of any care for him but because of how it impacts *you*."

I still believe most people's encouragement for forgiveness is about themselves, not those who have been victimized. These individuals want to live in a world where bygones are left behind and all is well. Their encouragement of forgiveness is for their own comfort.

But rape is not and never will be comfortable. I will never condone or forget what happened.

Over time, however, I have come to see how my anger toward Dickhead—and, to some extent, my school system and the police—was hurting me, the rage coursing through my body causing me to physically and mentally suffer.

So I work hard to slowly minimize my anger toward all of these groups. I am far from perfect on this. But I have already come a long way and believe I can go even further in the years to come.

# Letting Go

"You ready?" I ask.

My mom and I are pulling up to Katrina's house—except this time I am in the driver's seat, and she is on the passenger side. She looks nervous as she says, "I think so, but we'll see."

"Not everyone has a gang rape survivor, a kid with autism, and a husband with cancer for family members," I say with a laugh as she gets out of the car. "If that isn't a sign from somewhere above, I don't know what is."

My mom gives me a wry smile but doesn't say anything. She waves goodbye to me from Katrina's front door.

My mom did not have an easy childhood. But while it took her a couple of days to physically recover, her MDMA experience was different, and—in her characterization—much more positive than mine.

It meant so much to me that she decided to do MDMA. I saw it as a show of support for the work I was doing and that she was open to growing and changing, just as I was.

There were obviously a bunch of issues between us during my childhood. Even as an adult, I didn't feel like she took my pelvic problems seriously enough at the beginning. There was judgment from her when I first started using psychedelics and things were getting worse for me.

But she stepped up when I told her I had been raped. She never doubted me for a second or tried to make any of it seem like it was my fault. I know my situation stung her and led to some tough realizations, but at least when she was around me, the entire focus was about how I was going to get through this.

While I have the strongest of intentions to never have anything remotely like this happen to my hypothetical child, if, god forbid, something did occur, my intention would be to support them the way she has supported me through it.

My dad continued to frustrate me in the period after the rapes came up. While he would occasionally apologize that these still mostly unsaid things had happened, it felt like he was saying sorry I had randomly been struck by lightning rather than anything to do with him.

In his one visit to Austin, shortly after I started doing mushrooms and was struggling hard, he didn't get what I was going through at all. He seemed to think his purpose for being there was for me and the friends he had in town to show him a good time. The visit did not go well, and at one point, I screamed at him over things that had been boiling inside me for a while and kicked him out of my car.

While he knew I had gone to the police and sent the public letter about Dickhead, we never discussed it. There was a disconnect in that I did not think it was my job to keep him up to date or to ask him to support me, and he did not offer.

The frustration came to a head when, unsolicited, he advised me to write this book anonymously to avoid any reputational blowback. While he claimed this was out of concern for me and my career, I felt it had much more to do with his own shame, even if he could not see it.

But he did eventually come around. As the months went on, he sometimes sent positive texts indicating he was thinking about me.

The following Thanksgiving, we go for another walk.

"There are things I would have done differently," he says. "I can't change the past, but I do feel like we let you down."

"I appreciate you saying that," I reply. "If you guys really did that bad a job, given everything else I had going on, I never would have made it."

We both chuckle a little bit at that.

"I don't always show it well, but I do feel horrible for you. I love you and am proud you are my son."

"I know," I say back. "I love you too."

While it took a long time, I heard what I wanted to hear from him on this. He even commended me on writing this book and encouraged me to be as honest as possible in it, even about him. So I have been.

There will always be scars between me and my parents, especially with my dad. But I do love him in my own way and always will.

It's my tenth session. The second I put the mask on, I know it is go time.

I take five grams of psilocybin today, trying to push myself, but also not wanting to blow myself up.

The anticipation once I've taken the mushrooms is, in some ways, the worst part—listening to the music, every part of me knowing it is going to start getting hard very soon.

Waiting for the medicine to come on, my mind wanders. My family, my friends, what the future might look like, things in my past I have not thought about in a while.

But as the mushrooms start to hit, it comes back to the rapes, like a maze that has different routes only to end in the exact same spot.

And then, even though I feel cogent in my mind, I lose the ability to communicate verbally and all sense of what is going on outside me.

I start gagging, the same way I gagged on him.

At first, it feels like an exorcism. My whole body is revolting, like I am constipated, straining to get this bad energy out.

But as the chokes get more pronounced, I get into a rhythm, getting rid of this toxic imprint forever, the same way I would by throwing up or taking a dump.

It starts to almost feel *good*, the endorphins coming on the way they do from intense exercise.

As I keep going, I hear Katrina in the background. "It is just feelings, just energy, I am right here if you need me."

As I gag over and over, I can tell I am letting go of not one but many times I had his dick in the back of my mouth, maybe even all the times.

And then, at some point, I reorient and realize I have stopped making these horrible noises.

The emotions do not come for a long time, but they arrive with intensity when they do.

I start making sound again. Except as it is coming out, it doesn't sound like my voice at all. It is much higher. So high and so fast it is almost incoherent. "Mom-mom-mom-mom-mom," and after what feels like an eternity, it switches to, "Dad-dad-dad-dad," in the same rapid fire.

Most of the mushroom experience is internal. When sentences do come out, it is because I am struggling to work through these horrible feelings on my own and have to come up for air for a second.

The feelings of shame are some of the hardest. They keep coming up over and over, like a bottomless pit of garbage. There are so many of them that I can tell they will not all be moved through today, not even close. At a rough point, I again yell, "I want to die!"

"Do you really want to die, or do you just want the pain to stop?" Katrina asks. After thirty seconds of my silence, she remarks, "It is not coming out with nearly the same juice today. It is starting to sound like you don't really believe it."

Even through the mask, I can tell she is grinning.

At other times, I panic out loud that my pelvis will never heal, that I hate my body. And just like with the shame there is a seemingly endless supply of where these emotions are coming from, that I am just opening the door to how violated I feel.

But there is one moment when Katrina asks, "What is one thing you like about your body?"

After having to think about it, I decide on my smile, and she agrees.

As I say it out loud, it feels like I am seeing my smile in a whole new way. And it occurs to me that maybe my smile isn't so bad after all.

I see Dickhead power walking around my school, as he often did that second grade year, and feel the fear I felt then. The terror that he was around every corner even when he wasn't. That I could not escape him. But as I am shaking and breathing through these feelings of intense fear, there also comes an acceptance that I went to go find him for months and as I keep breathing, I swear I can feel my nervous system calming down, like a clock being reset.

And then, like all feelings, good or bad, they pass. My adrenaline is still pumping, but I can tell the mushrooms are starting to wear off a bit.

Even as I am coming down, the residual emotions continue to pour out of me. At one point, tears begin streaming down my face, and I say, "I just feel like I don't matter."

Katrina sighs. "Alex, I get how the little kid in you could believe that after what happened. And I am truly sorry that people were not there for you when you needed them. But *you* were there for you!" She says this with a force that surprises me.

"And I promise you matter. I've seen you matter to your family. It sure seems you matter to your friends. And you absolutely matter to me."

"I just want to be normal," I say, still sad.

Katrina sighs again. "I am not going to lie to you. You aren't going to be normal. And no matter how much psychedelics or healing you do, you will have major scars from this. But it is what you or anyone else chooses to do with their wounds after they turn to scars that counts.

"And over time, as you process and move through all the muck, even the horrible thing with those guys, there won't be as much emotional charge behind it anymore. It will fade, until one day it will seem like it happened to a different version, an old version of you.

"I think you are also going to get positives from this. You're going to have empathy, an emotional depth to you that most people who weren't in your situation don't have."

She shifts gears and starts clapping. "'I want to die' was a phase you had to go through, but you really started to go beyond that today and start working through the deeper feelings. There is plenty of work to do, but this was a big step in the right direction!"

I am still exhausted but calming down and getting coherent enough to speak in complete sentences.

"I wouldn't wish this shit on anyone," I say. "It definitely changed my life trajectory for the worse. But I guess it has led to a lot of growth too."

Katrina looks at her phone and then opens her blinds a tad. "It looks like your mom is outside. Chester is ready. I think it is about time for our walk."

After another minute of us sitting there, I finally say, "I do love you, you know."

"I love you too, Alex."

And then it is time to take my mask off, still smacked, and walk into the Texas sun with my three biggest supporters on the journey of a lifetime.

# Epilogue

keep doing psychedelics and the integration around them. After several more mushroom sessions, I feel better than before but, in many ways, still stuck, falling back into the same patterns—the shame, the anger, the lack of empathy, the vigilance, especially as I get further away from a session. My dick is still not working well at all.

Toward the end of one mushroom trip, a little more than eighteen months into my psychedelic journey, I decide it is time to move on for now, in just the same way as MDMA.

I still believe my pelvic floor issues have more to do with blunt-force trauma than anything related to sex. I repeatedly dismiss Katrina's suggestion that I could have that much fear or shame around it or that I go see a sex and intimacy coach.

I decide to switch to LSD+MDMA combined. LSD is a clear step up from the mushrooms and harsh, disorienting, and boundary shattering. In what will be the last of the repressed abuse, it comes up on LSD that the same crazy babysitter who hit me also sexually abused me in all the grossest ways possible, many times while giving me a bath.

When the memories and the gagging on her vagina come back, all my fears and shame around sex come tumbling out with it. I start yelling, "I hate sex," in much the same way I once shouted that I wanted to die. I go into a panic that if my pelvis loosens up, I will then have to have sex.

It comes in how much fear there is around sex for me. Even thinking about it feels gross, like there is something wrong with me for wanting it. It is impossible for me to imagine a consensual and positive sexual interaction, one that is not something to hide or be embarrassed about. Subconsciously, I've been feeling a deep fear and shame around sex my whole life. And in many ways, I am still stunted as a little kid when it comes to the topic.

The revelation around my babysitter did not change my life the way Dickhead did. When she came up, I'd already been working through the feelings around being serially sexually abused. But I do think it played a big role in my ongoing sexual dysfunction and at times hostility toward women. And that being violated at such an early age made me even more susceptible to further abuse.

My two experiences with LSD are as transformative as any of my MDMA or mushroom sessions. But they are also disconcerting enough compared to my other psychedelic experiences that, after two sessions, I am done. I got what I needed.

Afterward, when I go back to MDMA and mushrooms, it is a much different experience than before.

As I keep doing sessions and clearing out more of my trauma, I have the beginnings of a spiritual awakening. For me, believing in something bigger than myself has proven to be a large part of my healing journey. It's also given me more of an acceptance and less fear around death.

I also throw up the white flag and find an intimacy coach in Austin. Working with her is awkward and very hard for me at first.

But over time, I have gotten more and more comfortable in there, to the point where it is now *almost* fun.

These days, I am still working through the deepest feelings of sadness, shame, and vigilance, particularly around my body.

I wanted to announce that my body had completely recovered by the end of this book, even thinking about delaying the publication so that could be the case.

I am going to the bathroom much less, especially in the middle of the night. And, to keep it real, jacking off and shitting is much less painful than it used to be. But I am still dealing with muscle tension throughout my body, especially in my pelvis.

I decided to be honest about where I am now because I think it is just another example of how debilitating childhood sexual abuse can be.

Who knows—if there is ever a second edition of this book, perhaps I will update this section.

As of this writing, I have done twenty psychedelic sessions, nine predominantly MDMA, nine psilocybin, and two predominantly LSD, with ayahuasca on deck (I am not counting the ketamine). I would not be where I am today without all three of these compounds. But I only needed those three to work through the vast majority of my childhood trauma.

At the beginning, I had no idea why I was doing psychedelics. Then it became all about how I could get my dick to work correctly. But it evolved into something much bigger than that.

There was not one moment where everything flipped, which was a mistaken impression I had. I am not permanently blissful now, or even close to that. I still struggle with the desires, disappointments, and insecurities that I think all humans have on some level. But I no longer feel that life is inherently unfair or loathe myself the way I unconsciously did before psychedelics.

There will be a time when I decide my body has recovered. I have already scaled back some of my therapy and continuing to scale back will be another milestone for me. But I don't believe I will ever be fully "healed," in the same way I will never be perfect.

However, I am starting to move forward and am beginning to turn the page on this chapter of my life. The hardest parts of my journey were the events covered in this book, and I am confident they are behind me.

There will always be challenges and things to work through. But I also want to relax a little bit too. Maybe even pick up some hobbies—probably not the piano, though.

Psychedelics were just tools for me to do the work of beginning to heal myself. But I think without them, I was pretty much fucked. I guess there could have been antidepressants to take or other therapies to try that maybe would have helped around the edges and allowed me to "manage" everything. But I was so shut down and such a mess when I started doing medicine.

For me, trying to heal without psychedelics would have been like trying to unclog a toilet with my bare hands.

Choosing to use psychedelics to heal from childhood sexual abuse was the most important decision I ever made and the best thing I have ever done for myself.

As this book comes to a close, I am still seeing Katrina regularly. Once I began doing psychedelics and realized real change was possible, I desperately wanted someone who could push and help me grow. For me, more than anyone else, Katrina is that person.

Like everyone, Katrina has flaws, and in working with her up close for so many hours, I've seen those flaws just as she's seen mine. But I will always admire the dedication and commitment she brings to her craft and how she serves her clients.

She, along with my mom, was the most important person in getting me through this.

I suspect we will always have a "sharper" back and forth on certain things and even hurt feelings on occasion. But beneath the surface, it is all love.

I no longer like to profess hope for things I have some control over, so it is my intention she remain a friend and mentor for life.

As this book is going to print in 2024, Dickhead's name remains on his school's website as a current faculty member. Who knows what, if anything, will happen there. I don't pretend to be indifferent, but it also does not drive me the way it used to.

At this point, I see continuing to make the effort to hold him accountable as similar to taking out the trash or going to the dentist—something that makes sense to do, but not to get worked up about.

Whatever happens, I am going to be fine.

There will always be a scar the way I was dismissed. But sending that letter was one of the most important moments in my healing journey. It continues to bring a deep sense of satisfaction that I doubt will ever go away.

So while I would change certain things about how I chose to come forward, I would not change the decision to do so.

Initially, I was furious at both my parents for failing to protect me and a litany of other things during my childhood. As time has passed and I have done more of my own work, I still don't think they did a great job.

But there were positives to how they raised me as well. My mom modeled a raw determination and my dad a love to learn, especially through reading. And they both modeled a strong sense of personal integrity.

The same freedom that almost got me killed at eight years old later taught me to think for myself and gave me a strong sense of self-reliance.

I learned from them that if I felt something was right for me, I didn't have to ask for anyone's permission or approval, whether that was using psychedelics, sending that letter, or writing this book.

I will always be grateful for their financial support throughout my twenties, first in the doctors' visits and physical therapy appointments and later in the psychedelic sessions, the integration around it, and this book.

But most importantly, I do feel like I was loved growing up. Not the way I wanted or in some ways needed, but it was absolutely there in some form. And that made all the difference.

So far, I have done every single one of my psychedelic sessions in the United States. The time is now to start mainstreaming therapeutic psychedelics into American culture.

A day will come when there will be clinics all across this country, where after an intake, therapists can easily prescribe MDMA and psilocybin therapy with trained guides, the way they now prescribe SSRIs.

I believe with every bone in my body that psychedelics healing all kinds of trauma will be one of the positive stories of the twenty-first century.

No one gets to pick the family they were born into. But I am confident that every survivor can find someone who loves and cares about them deeply, who is willing to go above and beyond in helping them work through their trauma and go on to live a better life, like Katrina, Mrs. Hill, and Bruce all did for me.

The reality is rape is a dark but core part of the human experience. Whether of children or not, it has been going on as long as humans have been around. It will never truly stop or end. But for those like me who have had the misfortune of being sexually abused, I do think there is hope.

Because love is also a core part of the human experience.

And neither love nor psychedelics are going anywhere.

# Appendix A: My Interview

You can watch excerpts of my police interview on my website at traumaandecstasy.com/interviews or by scanning this QR code:

# Appendix B:
# The Letter

Dear Parents,

My name is Alex Abraham. I attended [my elementary school] from 2000–2006, starting in first grade. I am contacting you regarding former [my elementary school] music teacher and [his current school] teacher, "Mr. Bishop." Mr. Bishop sexually abused me throughout my first and second grade years, both in my home while he provided private piano lessons and in his classroom at [my elementary school]. I am writing to you now to make you aware of this serious situation. The County Police Department have been working on my case since late December 2021 and the School District was immediately notified of the allegations. Bishop has denied the accusations. However, I am 100 percent certain, beyond any doubt whatsoever, that Bishop raped me many times. As background, Bishop advertised in the school newsletter and my parents hired him for private piano lessons in my home during first grade.

Early on, Bishop offered to drive me home from school to avoid waiting for the bus. He drove me home frequently over the next two years. Bishop was extremely friendly, buying me gifts, offering me treats, and complimenting me on my piano skills. I now know Bishop was "grooming" me.

During an early lesson where my parents were home, Bishop fondled me over my shorts. The first time my parents were not home during a lesson, Mr. Bishop suggested we try something on the floor and he raped me in my living room. He said it was "our secret" and not to tell anyone. I didn't. He raped me several more times during my first-grade year both when my parents were not home during lessons and in his car while driving me to my house.

Over time, Bishop changed tactics and began to choke me after abusing me. He told me that "everyone would hate me" and he would "kill me" if I told anyone about the abuse. I didn't, as I was terrified. Over a period of months, the abuse at my home evolved into abuse at school. Mr. Bishop would find me during the after-school period when students dispersed and were waiting for the bus. Bishop would put his hand on my shoulder and direct me to his classroom where he raped me and forced me to give him oral sex. Sometimes, I hid from him.

Each time I did so, the next time he found me he would choke me and say if I ever hid from him again, he would kill me. Toward the end of my second grade year, Bishop arrived at my house for a piano lesson when my parents were not home. I refused to let him in and yelled through the door that I was going to tell my parents. Bishop broke into my house through the back deck door. He aggressively choked me and left. Shortly thereafter, he told my mother that he could no longer give me piano lessons, and the abuse ended. In December 2021, Mr. Bishop admitted to the police that he provided me with private music lessons and drove me home.

He also confirmed that he provided private music lessons to other students during this time frame. After elementary school, I graduated from a local private high school and then from [my university]. I now live in Austin, Texas, am employed and financially stable. In recent years, I have battled anxiety and depression as well as significant pelvic floor dysfunction. Through intensive therapy and pelvic floor work over the past six months, my repressed memories of these events have come flooding back and are now very clear.

Since I met with the police more than twelve weeks ago and [the school district] was notified, no one affiliated with [school district] has contacted me in any way. To my knowledge, Bishop remains employed and continues to be in daily contact with children at [his current elementary school].

I recognize these are extremely serious allegations. I would not make them, go to the police, or write to you unless I was certain beyond a doubt that I was raped and violently abused by Mr. Bishop. I have no hidden motive in coming forward. My hope is to hold Bishop accountable for his actions, to support others who may have been abused by Bishop, and to help other children avoid this awful experience.

Sincerely,
Alex Abraham

*Author's Note: While I did mention The Worst One in graphic detail to the police, I chose not to include it in the letter. I felt including it was not likely to change any minds and that the letter was strong enough without it.*

# Appendix C: Resources That Helped Me

*You can find links to all these resources at*
**Traumaandecstasy.com/Resources**

"My Healing Journey After Childhood Abuse" by Tim Ferriss and Debbie Millman (podcast)

"The Beginner's Guide to Psychedelics" and "What MDMA Did For Me" by Tucker Max (podcast and blog post)

*A Dose of Hope: A Story of MDMA-Assisted Psychotherapy* by Dan Engle and Alex Young (book)

*How To Do the Work: Recognize Your Patterns, Heal From Your Past and Create Your Self* by Nicole LePera (book)

*The Body Keeps The Score: Brain, Mind and Body in the Healing of Trauma* by Bessel van der Kolk (book)

*Victim No Longer: The Classic Guide for Men Recovering from Sexual Child Abuse* by Mike Lew (book)

*A Headache in the Pelvis: The Wise Anderson Protocol for Healing Pelvic Pain* (book) and accompanying *New York Times* article: https://www.nytimes.com/2013/12/31/health/a-fix-for-stress-related-pelvic-pain.html

*Healing Back Pain: The Mind-Body Connection* by John Sarno (book) and accompanying *New York Times* article: https://www.nytimes.com/2021/11/09/well/mind/john-sarno-chronic-pain-relief.html

*How to Change Your Mind: What the New Science of Psychedelics Teaches Us About Consciousness, Dying, Addiction, Depression, and Transcendence* by Michael Pollan (book)

*I Feel Love: MDMA and the Quest For Connection in Fractured World* by Rachel Nuwer (book)

*Letting Go: The Pathway of Surrender* by David Hawkins (book)

# Acknowledgments

I want to thank Skyler Gray; my cover designer, Anna Dorfman; my publishing managers, KT Leota and Lily Wood; my author strategist, Miles Rote; and everyone else at Scribe Media.

I am eternally grateful to my Austin-based practitioners, MCL, RL, and AA.

I want to thank my entire survivor group at Austin Counseling and Trauma Specialists.

I want to thank my entire extended family for their support, especially my uncle John Hartmann and my cousin Jeffrey Snyder.

I want to thank many of my coaches for their support during high school, particularly Rory Perkins, Nic Savage, and Rico Reed.

I want to thank many, although certainly not all (ha ha), of my teachers. I want to give particular shoutouts to Maddie Krug and Jeff Sealy for their encouragement of my writing.

I want to thank Andy Rehberger for being my first friend in middle school and being as cool as a cucumber, Nick Bazzarone for being my kindest friend, Robert Rucks for his infectious enthusiasm as well as for being my earliest friend to read and support this book, Matt Koger for being my favorite intellectual sparring partner and for his humor, Kevin McNerney for his consistent vibes as well as for providing me endless sports entertainment. Harrison Gray for his discipline and for picking me up that one night, Jesse Anderson for his laugh, and JJ Becker for his creativity as well as for continuing to be irrelevant in our fantasy league. I also want to thank Claudia d'Ottillie for her support and for being half of my favorite couple to third wheel with.

I want to thank Brandon Alden, Oliver De Thier, and Parth Verma for being my oldest friends. Even when everything around us changes, our dynamics always seem to stay the same. I also want to thank Zach Sekel and Nick Malpede for joining along the way.

I want to thank Nadine El Ashkar for her friendship on SAS and hosting me in Egypt.

I also want to thank many of my friends' families for their support over the years. I want to give particular shoutouts to the Bazzarone family for hosting me on multiple Christmases and many dinners, the McNerney family for frequently hosting me at their house and at their river house, and the Alden family for frequently hosting me at their home as well as at their beach house.

I want to give the biggest thank you to the Rehberger family. I will always be grateful for the love and support you guys have shown me over the many dinners, basement hangouts, holidays, and vacations.

Last but not least, I want to thank my two siblings. My sister Carly, who I often think is the only sane and normal one of all of us. And despite never wanting to take my phone calls, I want to thank the person I love most in the world, my brother Dan, for being himself.

# About the Author

M y author website is traumaandecstasy.com.
I am also starting a nonprofit to help people pay for psychedelic treatments, called Psychedelic Pathways; you can find more information on my website.

If you have any questions or are looking for a referral to anyone mentioned in the book, please get in touch with me via email. I can be reached at alex@traumaandecstasy.com or alex.l.abraham on Instagram.